Autobiography

Lori Ann Moeszinger

Total Surrender
My Story

By Lori Ann Moeszinger

Memoir
The Secrets of Prayer
When Death Knocked at My Door: The 5 Moments that Changed My Life
A Narrative Nonfiction Work

Autobiography
Total Surrender: My Story
and Your Blueprint for a Meaningful Life

Christian Living Series
Passion for Christ: New Beginnings

The Living Waters Series
Faith On Trial: The Startling Reality of Genuine Belief
Drenched in Faith: The Transformative Act of Water Baptism
Spirit Filled Life: The Unseen Force of Divine Power
The Bible Unbound: Trust, Translation, and Transformation
Prophets and Pulpits: Discerning Truth in the House of God
Beyond the Tithe: The Transformative Power of Generous Faith
Heart of Abundance: The Journey to Radical Giving and Receiving
Heaven's Reach: Drawing the Unbelieving into the Fold
Breaking Silence: The Charge to Uphold the Faith Out Loud
Beyond the Final Breath: The Christian's Voyage into Eternity

Christian Living Series
In Sacred Conversation: The New Testament Prayer Guide

Autobiography

Lori Ann Moeszinger

Total Surrender:
My Story
and Your Blueprint for a Meaningful Life

By

Lori Ann Moeszinger

Urban Chronicles Publishing House
an imprint of The Ridge Publishing Group
Coeur d'Alene, Idaho, U.S.A.

Library of Congress Control Number: 2024916245

Moeszinger, Lori Ann
Total Surrender: My Story and Your Blueprint for a Meaningful Life by Lori Ann Moeszinger

ISBN: 978-1-956905-02-1 (e-book)
ISBN: 978-1-956905-03-8 (softcover)

1. Biography & Autobiography / Personal Memoirs. 2. Religion / Christian Life/ Inspirational. 3. Self-Help / Spiritual. 4. Christian Life / Personal Growth. 5. Religion / Spirituality. I. Title.

First Edition: August 2024

Printed in the United States of America

Contents

Acknowledgments

I am forever indebted to our Lord Jesus Christ who worked so hard to get my attention. For years, I struggled to find my true purpose in life—like so many others. While in college, I found myself questioning if I was wasting my life, because my actions didn't reflect a life I was too proud of. I knew what I was passionate about—learning and teaching others what I learned—but I didn't know if following my passion aligned with God's purpose for my life. Finally, in 2016, out of complete and utter despair, I surrendered myself to the Lord not knowing what to expect! And from that day on, He's led me on a journey filled with discovery—getting to know Him—ultimately, finding my true purpose in life; answering God's call!

Thank you, again, Lord Jesus Christ for always being there in my life and being forever patient with me. For this I am humbled and truly grateful to be called not only a child of God but an ambassador of God. Praise God! Amen!

"Total Surrender: My Story and Your Blueprint for a Meaningful Life" challenges readers to lay down their lives in the full expression of faith. This compelling read calls for complete devotion to Christ, encouraging believers to relinquish control and trust in the divine path laid out for them. Through poignant narratives and scriptural insights, this book inspires a life lived wholly for God, fostering a deeper, more meaningful Christian walk.

Join Our Community

Engage more deeply with your faith by joining our vibrant community across several platforms:

- **Facebook Page**: Follow Guardians of Biblical Truth on Facebook for updates and community discussions that inspire and challenge.
- **Facebook Group**: Become a member of our exclusive group, Guardians of Biblical Truth Forum, for in-depth discussions and a supportive environment to share your journey of faith.
- **Blog**: Explore our blog at Jesus-Says.com for insightful posts and devotionals that delve into the complexities of scripture and personal surrender.
- **Social Media**: Stay connected and motivated by following us on X, Instagram, and Pinterest @NNSBible, where we share daily verses, reflections, and encourage community interaction.

We're excited to support and interact with you as you explore the depths of your faith!

Autobiography

Lori Ann Moeszinger

Total Surrender
My Story

Introduction

Finding your true purpose in life—our reason for existence—is simply to be in a relationship with our Creator God.

How do we do this?

First, we need to acknowledge that God exists in all of His forms: God the Father, God the Son, and God the Holy Spirit—our God is three persons in One which makes up the Godhead also called the Holy Trinity. For all of eternity—past, present, and future—the Father, the Son, and the Holy Spirit have always been in relationship and communication with each other.

The Bible says, "For from Him and through Him and to Him are all things" (Romans 11:36).

Second, we need to understand that our true purpose in life is to follow God's plan by serving our Lord Jesus Christ. God is the reason we exist. He is the one that gave us all the precious gift of life. Life is not about paying attention to our own self-absorbed, self-serving, and self-interested wants and needs. It's not about our goals. And it's not about the things we accumulate. It's about paying attention to God! It's about becoming the person He wants us to be during this lifetime. Likewise, we are not following our true purpose in life—our calling in life—without the Lord in our life. But with Him in our life, we'll find blessings are abundant!

> "Therefore I, a prisoner for serving the Lord, beg you to lead a life worthy of your calling, for you have been called by God. Always be humble and gentle. Be patient with each other, making allowance for each other's faults because of your love. Make every effort to keep yourselves united in the Spirit, binding yourselves together with peace" (Ephesians 4:1–3).

When I began my journey to know God and to understand the messages of the Bible, I was careful not to identify with any specific religion or manmade religious doctrines. I wasn't interested in man's opinion when it came to matters of the Holy Scriptures. In fact, my only interest was and is in the Word of God, the Bible unaltered—God's written Word and messages to humankind.

As I poured over my Bibles, study Bibles, extra-biblical works, CDs, DVDs, videos, and the occasional guest speaker talking points for the past decade, The Ridge Publishing Group and its imprint, Guardians of Biblical Truth and its New Narrated Study Bible (NNSB) is the result—the Bible told in a modern way.

If there was ever a time, when people need God in their lives, that time is now. We live in troubled times. Political, social, and economic corruptions are so prevalent in our daily lives; we often seem to be in danger of losing any sense of happiness or peace. And many people have lost touch with basic values and beliefs. Life is so serious for so many people and hard that they simply don't pause to discover the inner strength that comes through a relationship with our Creator God—the

Lord Jesus Christ. And so, with end times nearing, I can't help sense an urgency to save souls—that is the reason for my books.

> "Blessed is the one who reads aloud the words of this prophecy, and blessed are those who hear, and who keep what is written in it, for the time is near" (Revelation 1:3).

Invitation

After reading this far, I thank you. With that said, I never start a book without giving an opportunity for people to get right with God. It is really inescapable, the fact that the Bible does teach eternity—once we are born, we live forever. There really is a heaven. There really is a hell. And the Bible tells us that we are going to spend eternity in one of these two places. The choice is ours. God has already made His choice. God loves us. He sent His only Son, Jesus Christ, to die on a cross for the forgiveness of our sins.

> "For God so loved the world, that He gave His only begotten Son, Jesus Christ, that whosoever believes in Him should not perish (die) but have everlasting life" (John 3:16).

Because God is holy, we need to be holy through Jesus Christ. He will never change; He is immutable, unchangeable. He is in the total state of sinless perfection in everything that He does. But you and I are not holy. By nature, we are sinful and selfish. And because we are sinful and selfish, we are separated from a holy God. But God told us, we were created in His image, and it is His desire to redeem us to right relationship with Him. Therefore, Jesus is the bridge between the holiness of God and the unholiness of humanity. And the Bible also tells us that the only way to break the curse of sin and to find right relationship with God is through Jesus Christ.

"Jesus says unto him, I am the way, the truth, and the life: no man comes unto the Father, but by Me" (John 14:6).

The Gospel

The word "gospel" in the Greek original text means "good news of the kingdom of God." In Christianity, the term "good news" refers to the story of Jesus Christ's birth, ministry, death, and resurrection. Jesus Christ, the Son of God, died for our sins and rose again, eternally triumphant over His enemies—so that there is now no condemnation for those who believe but only everlasting joy. Wherefore the fullness of the gospel is in God Himself—enjoyed by His redeemed people.

Through the death, the ministry, the burial, and the resurrection of Jesus Christ, you and I not only have power over sin, but we have power over sickness, disease, and infirmity—yesterday, today, and forever. The same seven ways Jesus healed in the New Testament are still available to every believer today. Jesus Christ is still the great physician, and no weapon formed against His children shall prosper in the name of the Lord Jesus Christ.

> "But He was wounded for our transgressions (sins), He was bruised for our iniquities (immoral behavior): the chastisement (punishment) of our peace was upon Him; and with His stripes (the marks on His back from His beating) we are healed" (Isaiah 53:5).

> "Who His own self bore our sins in His own body on the tree (cross), that we being dead to sins, should live unto righteousness: by whose stripes you are healed" (1 Peter 2:24).

Making Peace with God

How do you make peace with God?

You have to do two things:

First, you must believe in the gospel—the teaching and revelation of Christ. The gospel, just as scriptures says: (1) Jesus Christ, God the Father's only Son, lived on this Earth, (2) died on a cross for the forgiveness of our sins, (3) was buried, (4) was raised from the dead on the third day, (5) stayed on this Earth for 40 days before ascending to heaven, (6) promised to return, and (7) we are saved by faith alone in Christ alone—this is called the doctrine of salvation.

Second, you must receive Christ by doing three things: (1) Recognize and admit your sins. The Bible says, "For all have sinned, and come short of the glory of God" (Romans 3:23). (2) Repent of your sins. Jesus said, "No, I tell you; but unless you repent, you will all likewise perish" (Luke 13:3). Repentance means you recognize your sins; you admit your life is headed in the wrong direction, and now you must be willing to turn your back on sin and turn your heart to Christ. (3) Receive Jesus Christ as your personal Lord and Savior. Commit your heart to Him by faith—in childlike faith; showing the good qualities that children have, such as trusting people, being honest and enthusiastic, expressing a childlike innocence or quality.

> "The Lord is not slack concerning His promise, as some men count slackness; but is longsuffering toward us, not willing that any should perish, but that all should come to repentance" (2 Peter 3:9).

That word "men" in the Greek is generic; it means "men and women." Therefore, if you have never recognized and repented of your sins (changed your carnal ways). If you've never had a relationship with

God. Or perhaps, you are backslidden or away from God or you've wandered. The Bible says, "I will heal your backsliding, I will love them freely: for My anger is turned away from him" (Hosea 14:4). You can come home to your heavenly Father today, and He will love you, and forgive you, and cleanse you, and strengthen you to be what He's called you to be.

It isn't by accident that you are reading this book. I believe the Lord by His leading and His mercy brought us together. And so, I want to ask you to pray the prayer of salvation—also called the prayer of faith and sometimes called the sinner's prayer—to make peace with God. Just, with a sincere heart, pray the prayer of salvation out loud in childlike faith and make a commitment right now.

Why out loud? Because Christ did everything publicly.

> "For whosoever shall be ashamed of Me and of My words, of him shall the Son of Man be ashamed, when He comes in the glory of His Father with His holy angels" (Luke 9:26; also in Mark 8:38).

And after you've done that, go to our website, The Ridge Publishing Group at https://www.RidgePublishingGroup.com, and click on "Subscribe Now," and I'll send you a special gift—a PDF copy of my book, "Passion for Christ: New Beginnings"; print and e-book copies are available at Amazon.com as well as at other bookstores and online resellers. Because this isn't the end of what God's going to do in your life, just the beginning, I'll also send you our monthly New Beginnings Newsletter.

> "Go therefore and make disciples of all nations, baptizing them in the name of the Father and of the Son and of the Holy Spirit, teaching them to observe all that I have

commanded you. And behold, I am with you always, to the end of the age" (Matthew 28:19–20).

Just pray this, out loud:

"Heavenly Father, today as I was reading the Bible, you were speaking to me. I want to be right with God. I recognize my sins and I ask for forgiveness. I believe Jesus Christ is your Son. I believe that He died on the cross as payment for sin and rose again as the hope of the world. And I recognize that Jesus is the only salvation and the only Savior available. In childlike faith, I trust in the Lord Jesus from this day forward. I repent of my sins, and I trust in the blood that was shed on the cross for the forgiveness of my sins. Cleanse me; my mind, my body, and my spirit. Come into my heart. And I vow this day, I will live for you all the days of my life. Guide my life and help me to do your will. Fill me with the Holy Spirit and give me the power to be what you want me to be. Be my Lord and Savior. According to the Bible which cannot lie, all who call upon the name of the Lord, shall be saved. Today, I'm saved. I'm forgiven. I'm delivered. I'm healed. The curse of sin and sickness and lack in my life are now broken. And I have become the righteousness of God through Jesus Christ. And I'll never be the same. I pray this in Jesus Christ's precious name. Amen."

The Bible said either your Father is God, or your father is the devil. And the Bible said that the power of sin and Satan comes to steal, and to kill, and to destroy. But Jesus said:

"The thief comes not, but for to steal, and to kill, and to destroy; I come that they might have life, and that they might have it more abundantly" (John 10:10).

Jesus is the master of life. And if you want to walk in the life of forgiveness and have that relationship with God the Father, you can begin that today. All you have to do is pray the prayer of salvation to make peace with God—in doing so, you become a born again Christian.

"Therefore if any man be in Christ, he is a new creature: old things are passed away; behold, all things become new" (2 Corinthians 5:17).

Total Surrender My Story is not just an autobiography about my call with God. It is a clarion call—a call to something that is hard to ignore. It is a wakeup call to all of humanity to choose God before it's too late. And get prepared for the second coming of Jesus Christ, our Lord and Savior—time is near, He is knocking at the door:

"Behold, I stand at the door and knock. If anyone hears My voice and opens the door, I will come in to him and eat with him, and he with Me" (Revelation 3:20).

When you know God and understand the wisdom of the Bible, it will change you! This is our calling—our true purpose in life. Let the Lord into your life; He has a plan . . . when you do that, amazing things start to happen: You'll become passionate about God. You'll begin to crave to think and speak in line with Jesus' ways. You'll start to see yourself the way Christ sees you. You'll habitually tune into the Holy Spirit, who lives within those in Christ, to check for a sense of peace in your choices. And then miracles begin to happen . . .

Part One

Total Surrender: My Story
Wisdom and Lessons

TOTAL SURRENDER

Why Am I Here?

Many people ask: What drove you to move to Northern Idaho? The short answer, God did. The longer answer is My Story herein.

Pleading with God

Living in Northern California—or the cement jungle as my husband calls it—my life seemed ordinary: By the time I was 56-years-old, I had three sons and was on my third marriage. I was educated; I had three degrees—an associate degree in paralegal studies, bachelor's degree in business administration, and Juris Doctorate in law. I had three career paths spanning fashion, high-tech, and publishing industries. I retired at age 47 to care for my husband's three parents before each successively passed away, and then moved on to caring for my own parents. We owned our own home, had a couple of cars, and were living the American Dream. Yet, something was wrong. I was becoming more and more restless, impatient and unhappy.

Then . . . one day, out of despair . . . I found myself throwing my arms up in the air, sobbing and pleading with God to give me a direction—I was miserable! (Although I have always believed in God, I hadn't reached out in a very long time . . . then there was that covenant that I had made with Him back in 2007—more about this later.)

And on that day . . . all of a sudden . . . I found myself overcome by stillness. I kind of stopped everything. The kids were grown and out of the house; it was just the three of us: my husband, our dog, and me. And I just sat still—something I had not ever purposefully done before.

I wasn't bored; but I found myself browsing the internet on YouTube. Again, this is something I had never done before. I was old school; I loved books and the library. Saying that I was "an information junky" would be stating the obvious. I thought I was interested in preparedness and found pastor Joe Fox's Viking Preparedness videos.

But then I wanted more. I knew I was also interested in learning about God and the Bible . . . but I didn't know where to start. My father was Mormon, my mother was Catholic, and so mom tried to raise my three brothers and I Christian. Along my discovery, I seemed to be drawn to pastor Steve Cioccolanti's end times videos. And I was hooked!

My husband, not a believer nor a non-believer, thought I was nuts; so I backed off the videos. He was tired of hearing pastor Steve in the background night after night; and he thought I was becoming a bit obsessed. I, however, wouldn't call it obsession, but rather my newfound passion for Christ! So I put my best argument forward:

"Well, I don't believe in non-believers . . ." Even so, I stopped watching the videos . . .

God's Message—Move!

Over the next couple of weeks, again, I found myself anxious. Although we lived in an exclusive setting in the Bay Area called Santana Row, I suddenly had become very aware of all the sin and wickedness around me, and it felt like it was consuming me. It was too convenient to go downstairs to the bars and restaurants and overindulge, crime was at an all-time high, and not being accountable for your actions seemed to be the new normal.

Then it dawned on me: It wasn't just Santana Row, or the reasons why I pulled our kids out of the public school system, or the injustice of our current legal system. It was what the state of California had become—a socialist, sanctuary state, which had little interest in culpability. I needed to move! I wanted out of California. All of a sudden, I could hear God loud and clear. Move!

But where would we move to? Both my husband and I were born and raised in California and had lived there much of our lives. Yes, I moved around the states and traveled quite a bit both domestically and abroad on cruises, and even owned timeshares in Maui and Kauai. But to narrow the question down, I initially knew three things: (1) We no longer had any interest in traveling outside of the United States because of the current state of world affairs. (2) Hawaii never interested me, simply because I didn't want to live an ocean away from our sons, which would also eliminate Alaska. (3) New York, Chicago, Las Vegas, and Florida were also out—too many people, too much crime, too hot, and too many bugs—been there, done that. So there it was in black and white; I had reduced my search down to 43 states.

So, yep, I turned back to YouTube videos and started listening to pastors Steve Cioccolanti and Joe Fox's videos again. The former kept my appetite for God satisfied. While the latter was my go to videos for relocation possibilities. Pastor Joe Fox had settled in the Arkansas Ozarks. He was a former Special Forces soldier who wrote the book, "Survival Family: Prepared Americans for a Strong America"—your go-to guide for staying safe in an unsafe world. Of course, I bought the book. So I initially thought, maybe the Ozarks . . . but was preparedness really my path? Was God speaking to me?

Once more, I felt I needed to do more discovery to get more answers. I was only interested in 43 continental states. So I queried: What are the best states to live in? As I continued to watch videos, I came across Joel Skousen's videos. He wrote the book, "Strategic Relocation: North American Guide to Safe Places"—yes, I bought the book. In the book, he shows a table at the beginning of each state with a summary of facts, ratings and overall star approval for the state, including: climate, population demographics, cost of living index, private land availability, building permits, land and urban planning, food production, health environment, traffic, politics, taxes, corruption, crime, personal liberty, gun liberty, alternative medicine, home schooling, and military targets. Only two states had a four star rating: Montana and Wyoming; and two states had a five star rating: Idaho and Utah.

Although it was my early intention to visit all four of these states, I found myself drawn towards Idaho—specifically, Northwest Idaho. We had two grown sons and a grandson that lived just across the border in Spokane, Washington. We had visited Spokane many times before but were never interested in relocating there; it felt, too much, like an up and coming California. Northern Idaho, on the other hand, seemed promising; coincidently, we had long-term family friends—Mark and Stacey, our middle son's godparents—who lived in Post Falls, North Idaho. And I don't believe in coincidences; this was clearly another sign from God!

And then, all of a sudden, I found myself calm once again. I had a new direction: I knew I wanted out of California and I sensed Northern Idaho was going to be the answer. If not, we'd travel to Utah, Montana, and Wyoming as well.

Along my journey, I quickly learned two things: (1) the more I surrendered to God and followed God's plan, things just simply fell into place—and my validation was always a calm state. However, (2) whenever I'd get complacent or head down a wrong path, the opposite would happen—my anxiety would surely soar. Unfortunately, this new life changing revelation, took me 50-something years before I finally got it; often hitting wall after wall despite all of my successes.

God's Intervention

My husband, though, was not so sure. He wasn't sure he wanted to leave California. He was a highly sought after engineer, working in the heart of Silicon Valley, and had a great job . . . but then, without warning, he was suddenly out of a job. He and his engineering team had been working with a new employer; the new employer—nine months earlier—had acquired the company he had been employed at for many years. Nevertheless, a few months later, the new employer decided to get out of the new business and chose to layoff him and his entire team. He was dazed—it caught him completely off guard.

The good news, he received a six-month severance package! He might have been temporarily bummed. Me, I was excited! I found this was another sign from God! In my mind, that gave us a couple of months to travel, and North Idaho was at the top of the list. But first, we would share our windfall with our family and friends: our first destination, we took my parents to the Wynn Las Vegas and Encore Resort. We then continued on—just the two of us—to our timeshare in Princeville, Kauai. Following Kauai, we headed for our timeshare in Kaanapali, Maui where we hosted our friends, Duane and Barbara, and Scott and Susan. Our last stop would be Coeur d'Alene, Idaho; where we would meet up with Mark and Stacey.

But there would be a setback . . .

Am I On the Right Path?

A few nights before we were supposed to leave our timeshare in Maui, and venture to Northern Idaho, my husband told me he didn't want to go—he just wasn't interested in moving at all. In fact, he always wanted to retire with the company he'd started his career with in Sunnyvale, California, which he called his dream job; hence, all the more reason not to move. He had also mentioned his old boss that was still there— many times over the course of our marriage—so I told him to make the call. I always supported my husband's desires.

He made the call and afterwards, he felt like the prospect of him returning to Sunnyvale was very promising.

Later, he'd interview and get the job! Truly a blessing from God!

God Spoke to Me in a Dream

Then, that night changed everything—I had a dream. I told my husband about the dream the next morning.

"God came to me last night and said, 'he will fall in love and you will follow.'"

This puzzled me, I was sure it would happen the other way around: I would fall in love and he would follow. Now, he was intrigued. And I was convinced! Thank you, Lord Jesus Christ!

I immediately contacted Mark and Stacey in Post Falls. Post Falls is bounded by Coeur d'Alene to the east, Stateline and the state of Washington to the west, and the Spokane River to the south. But based on what I had learned from reading the book, "Strategic Relocation," I knew I did not want to live near a Stateline border.

We explained, we were interested in exploring Coeur d'Alene to possibly move there and we'd be coming into town shortly. Our friends didn't disappoint. They told us where to stay: the Coeur d'Alene Resort—downtown on the water. They told us not to rent a car: they would drive us around to show us the town. They even scheduled a real estate agent to take us house hunting.

Thankfully, my husband loves me very much and was in it for the long hall. He'd always say I was the best wife he'd ever had . . . but that's because I am the only wife he has ever had. He had been a bachelor for 40-years when I met him. Two years later, we were married—a single moment in time that would change my life. It wasn't until after we were married, when he told me, he much preferred the married life to the single life. Inasmuch, he understood, being happily married includes a life of compromises.

God's Country

A few days later, our flight was uneventful and touched down at the Spokane, Washington airport. Coeur d'Alene was just 45-minutes outside of Spokane. We had pre-arranged transportation with the Coeur d'Alene Resort to be picked up. They were right on schedule.

As we drove across the state borderline, I could see forest trees ahead. And I instantly fell in love with the trees! The trees! They were breathtaking! We definitely had entered into God's country.

When we pulled up to the Resort; it, too, was stunning! It hovered over Lake Coeur d'Alene with its many docks, sandy beaches, bridges, headquarters, and ticket booths: ferryboat cruises, seaplane tours, hang gliding excursions, paddle boarding, and much more. We had officially arrived in Paradise!

That evening, our sons and their entourage, met us at the Resort and joined us for dinner. They, too, were excited with the possibility of mom and step-dad moving so close to them. As for my husband and I, we were just thrilled to see the family again.

We had dinner at Dock Side, the Resort's casual dining restaurant, and then retreated to our suite. We knew we would have a large group spending time with us during our stay so we booked a full suite. The young ones loved hanging out on the terrace—so close to the water— watching and listening to the music of the boats docked just across the way. And before everyone left, the mini-bar snacks and drinks were nearly empty.

Before turning in for the evening, my husband and I enjoyed some rest and relaxation on our terrace as well. We both felt it. Coeur d'Alene gave us both an immediate sense of calm and belonging.

House Hunting with God

The next morning, we met up with the local real estate agent that our friend, Mark, had prearranged. Over the next few days, she'd take us from area to area, house to house, learning what we did and didn't like. My husband was annoyed—he still had no intention of moving—but I made sure we'd have plenty of "pub time," so he went along with my wishes. I even bought some time and patience by convincing Mark to tag along with us, at least for the first three days.

I wasn't sure how everything was going to turnout . . . but somehow . . . deep inside . . . I just knew a move to Idaho would happen . . .

On the fourth day, our realtor called us early that morning.

She explained, "now that I know what you are looking for, I need to take you to a new area—The Ridge at Cougar Bay."

The Ridge at Cougar Bay is a private, gated community with 77-home sites featuring wooded areas and breathtaking lake views—set up against acres of forest. Located just a couple of bird's eye miles, otherwise, a quick four mile drive to downtown Coeur d'Alene. The Ridge offers residents the best of both worlds: the convenience of city living in a charming, yet, rural setting.

I asked her, "how much were the homes?"

She answered, "a million plus."

I told her, "we need to pass—my husband would never sign up for spending a million plus on a home."

But she insisted, so I agreed.

As she drove us up the winding hill, the first home that came into view was a large home at the top of the hill. Then, as we continued up and around the hill, more and more homes and a few empty lots speckled in between came into sight. The development was only a few years old, so not all of the lots had homes.

We were stunned! We had been all over Coeur d'Alene but nothing compared to this area. And the views! Most of the home sites, sat directly—on a ridge—across the lake from the downtown Coeur d'Alene Resort; where we were staying.

And the homes! Each home was different from the other—all custom built—not a single home looked like the other.

She explained that The Ridge was a home owner's association (HOA) development and all owners had to adhere to the HOA Design Review Guidelines before seeking approval to build. In addition, only four builders had been approved to build on the sites.

We couldn't believe what we were seeing. Most of the homes seemed to be 5,000 to 6,000 square feet—some larger, a few smaller. Everywhere you looked, the landscaping was meticulous! This couldn't be real . . . As I pondered the impossibilities of it all . . . abruptly . . . my thought was interrupted.

My husband was shouting, "Stop! Stop!"

Our realtor looked at me.

And I said to her, "if he said, 'stop,' please do."

So she did.

As he got out of the car, I could see, he couldn't take his eyes off one of the empty lots we almost passed by. So I followed him. He walked to the edge of that lot and I could instantly see, he'd fallen in love with the view!

I hadn't seen that facial expression on his face, since our time in Maui, when he fell in love with a painting Anthony Hopkins had done—shortly after he found out he had cancer. We purchased that painting that day!

And he was right—the view was truly spectacular!

Not in my wildest dreams, could I have ever thought that The Ridge might be our future home site. Up until that moment, my husband was completely against the idea of moving out of California. Now, he had to have this lot!

So I asked her, "is the lot available for sale?

She said, "I'm not sure, but I don't think so."

So I pushed . . . she called her office on the spot and found out the lot was available. We were thrilled!

(Apparently, the lot had been purchased, perk tested, water hooked up—but just before the couple were about to break ground, they found out her husband had brain cancer. Shortly thereafter, he passed away and she had just put the lot back up for sale.)

We'd purchase the lot that same day for full ask. We figured the woman had been through enough; I wasn't going to haggle with her on the price.

And so it all happened, exactly how God said it would occur: in my dream, a few nights earlier, God told me, "he would fall in love and I would follow."

As I reflected back, I couldn't believe how strong my communication with God was becoming—simply by paying attention to Him. He was speaking to me and I was listening; I discovered I'd often get chills, a sign of God speaking to me.

And now, we were moving to Coeur d'Alene, Idaho!

Over the course of the last few months, I had discovered, I didn't need to know "the how" things were going to transpire—as long as I was following God's plan; not my own path, which always caused me anxiety. I just needed to have "faith" (to know) that things would happen in God's perfect timing, which always brought me a sense of calm, a sense of peace. After all, it is not in the miracle of it all, it is always in the timing of the miracle.

"What is impossible with man is possible with God" (Luke 18:27).

"I am the Lord, the God of all mankind. Is anything too hard for me?" (Jeremiah 32:27).

And when I followed God's plan, our blessings just kept coming:

- When I realized God wanted me out of California . . . God put me on a video path to pastors Joe Fox and Steve Cioccolanti.

- When I needed more direction, God put me on a video path to Joel Skousen, who led me to the state of Idaho.

- Then, shockingly, out of the blue, my husband was part of a layoff . . . God made time and money available for us to have the opportunity to travel and explore Idaho.

- My husband always had a deep longing to finish his career with the company he started at . . . God orchestrated his layoff to motivate him to make that call; and later, he'd get his dream job back.

- Following this, when my husband fell in love with the lot at The Ridge . . . God allowed history to repeat itself, and we'd purchase that lot the same day. At a low moment in his life, he fell in love with an original painting done by actor Anthony Hopkins; he purchased it that day.

"The thing that has been, it is that which will be; and that which is done is that which will be done: and there is no new thing under the sun" (Ecclesiastes 1:9).

But for, an unfortunate circumstance, that lot would not have just come back onto the market for sale . . . God, in his perfect timing, made that lot available for us to purchase that day.

Meanwhile, I couldn't help but wonder, what was next . . . suddenly, life seemed exciting again! I couldn't believe how happy I'd become in such a short time just because I surrendered myself to God's will—a single moment that would change my life forever.

When would we be moving to Coeur d'Alene?

I'd get my answer in God's perfect timing . . .

Architects, Builders, and Designers

3

In everything I was doing, surrendering to God's will—following God's plan; not my own plan or my husband's plan to stay in California—God was taking me on a journey to find my true destiny. He wanted us to move out of California. He wanted us to move to the state of Idaho. He wanted us to move to Coeur d'Alene, North Idaho, also referred to as Idaho's Panhandle: defined by numerous lakes, prairies and untouched wilderness. The region also has one of the most scenic mountain ranges in the state, and recreational activities abound. And now, He wanted us to move to The Ridge at Cougar Bay.

Closing the Deal

Later that day . . . after much paperwork . . . we were officially in contract to purchase our lot up at The Ridge. But apparently, our realtor wasn't done with us yet—I guess a "land sale contract" didn't compare to a home under contract. She wanted more.

That same day, she introduced us to her brother, who was a local architect, and his wife, who was an interior designer. During our meeting with her brother, he explained, he charges $0.60 per square foot. So if we were building a 5,000 square foot home, the cost would be $3,000 for an initial set of blueprints. However, if there were any changes thereafter, this would continue to drive the costs up.

I couldn't help but think to myself; of course there's going to be changes . . . I've never designed a house before! I prayed for a sign from God; if this was our path? I left his office feeling uneasy. Though, I was thankful for the insight.

Next, still that same day, our realtor also made arrangements for us to meet a highly sought after custom homebuilder, Rosenberger Construction. She was looking for an opportunity for her brother to work with Rosenberger, on behalf of a client, as the architect for the project. But that wasn't all . . . unbeknownst to us, this chain of events—her introducing us to Rosenberger Construction—could have set in motion an obligation for our builder to have to pay our realtor a commission—called buyer's representation—if he took us on as a client. She was playing on our ignorance . . . had we known this ahead of time, we would have never agreed to the introduction. It was all too much, and a little too pushy for me; but I played along anyway . . .

My husband, on the other hand, was biting his tongue; and yet, he was unusually patient with me. He thought meeting with a builder at this point and time was a waste of everyone's time. He had no intention of building a home anytime in the near future. Nor did he really ever entertain—in his mind—the idea of building a home at all in the future. He figured, since it was land, it would always be a good investment that he could sell at a later date. So I spun it into the idea that we were just collecting figures; to get an idea of how much it would cost to build a home on the lot. He played along . . .

Builder Hunting with God

For more than three decades, Rosenberger Construction has been building custom homes as the premier custom homebuilder in Coeur d'Alene, Idaho and the surrounding region. Our meeting was to be with Ron Rosenberger; from his website: Born and raised in Hayden (a city just outside of Coeur d'Alene), Ron started his career in construction humbly shoveling pea gravel in garages for a local general contractor. Laborer tasks became the gateway to a lifelong career in the trade and decades of hands-on experience in all facets of residential building, which sets him apart from his competition. Ron's eye for detail and unwavering commitment to quality in everything he does has shaped a company that offers a product and service widely regarded as one of the best. Approachable, knowledgeable and experienced, Ron's stamp on your project adds value from the start.

During our meeting with Ron, from the onset, it was obvious that our realtor was trying to take the lead. And her actions were really ramping up my husband's stress level; she'd become exhausting and relentless. But I'd been cutting her some slack, we may have been overwhelmed by the events of the day, but she was after all our transportation. Nonetheless, in defense of my husband, I quickly shut her down. Instead, I told her, I preferred Ron to take the lead and so he did . . .

He began by showing us a gallery of custom homes he had built; and I fell in love with the Lake House! Unfortunately for me, it was a 10,000 square foot home, which we could never afford . . . but the design would later become my obsession. He also pointed out some of his custom-signature details that he did to all of the custom homes he built, for instance, three-course fascia; layering the fascia adds depth and gives an effect like crown molding to the roof rim—a big visual upgrade over standard single fascia. Finally, he'd give us a brochure package, which included: his Classic and Signature Collection floor plans and features, a booklet with the Lake House on the cover, and a foldout brochure.

As I took a moment, browsing through the brochure package, I noticed that all his homes—Classic and Signature Collections—therein were traditional one- and two-story homes. I explained that our lot was on a slope so we wanted to build a home with a daylight basement. He told us, he does this all the time. In fact, he just happened to be building such a home up in the hills—so he invited us up to go take a look.

If God was answering my prayers for validation: Am I still on the right path? Will I be living in a home with a daylight basement? He couldn't have given me a clearer picture. As I mentioned before, I don't believe in coincidences; we were meant to build a home with a daylight basement on our lot! Or, would we?

Still, we were thrilled—we'd never been in a home with a daylight basement before. So we didn't hesitate to take Ron up on his offer. He then gave us the address before concluding our meeting. Once again, our realtor would be our wheels.

A Picture of a Daylight Basement

Next, our realtor kindly hauled us up to the site. As we toured the home, we couldn't help take in the grandness a daylight basement gave the home compared to a traditional two-story home.

Think of a daylight basement as a reverse two-story home: sometimes called a walk-out basement, it is contained in the house situated on a slope, so that part of the floor is above ground, with a doorway to the outside. The part of the floor lower than the ground can be considered the true basement area. From the street, the home appeared to be one story, but from the back—slope side—the home looked like a two-story home.

Once again, we felt very blessed with the possibilities of it all.

God Chooses Builder

Later that evening, my husband and I reminisced on the magnitude of the events of the day. This included: seeing The Ridge at Cougar Bay for the first time, noticing the home up on top of the hill, and finding the empty lot two parcels over; that lot being available for sale again; closing the deal; architect introduction and information; Rosenberger Construction meet and greet; and visiting the home under construction with the daylight basement.

At the end of the day, both my husband and I knew Rosenberger Construction would build our home. Not only do his projects exude beauty and quality, his craftsmanship can be compared to none other. For that, I am thankful that our realtor made this connection for us.

Later, we'd learn that The Ridge Design Review Guidelines recommended only four builders, and Rosenberger was one of them.

Thus, we would have come to the same conclusion with or without our realtor's introduction.

We were completely sold! But, it, too, like everything else—a pattern that I was now very familiar with—wouldn't come together exactly "how" we imagined it would . . .

Designing Our Dream Home

Back in California . . . my husband initially thought purchasing the land would appease me for at least the next five years—he'd tell me later. Not so, I had other plans. I was like a dog with a bone. I had found a new love and a new passion—we were following God's plan! We were moving to Coeur d'Alene, Idaho! And we were building a custom home at The Ridge at Cougar Bay—our dream home! Our forever home! And it would be a Rosenberger home!

So immediately, upon our return from Coeur d'Alene, I got started on my new project! First, I went online and reviewed Rosenberger Construction's website: who they are, their process, sub-contractor list, and gallery photos. (Later, we'd realize, many of the pictures on the website and in both the brochure booklet and foldout were of the Lake House and that first home we saw—at the top of the hill—when we initially drove up to The Ridge.) I'd snap screenshots of the website images I liked and started filling the pages of my new PowerPoint presentation—Moeszinger Home Build Project.

Next, I read through all of the Homeowners Association CC&Rs and Design Review Guidelines; I'd add these notes to my build management slides. Then, I logged into Amazon and ordered several books: "Designing Your Dream Home," "How to Build Your Dream Home without Getting Nailed!," "Super Natural Home," "Green

Home Building," "The Self-Sufficient Home" . . . I'd read each book cover to cover and added those notes to my slides as well.

Finally, with everything I learned, I started designing each individual space in what was to be our future home. But I wasn't designing just any home. I was designing our dream home, our forever home: (1) a home we could age-in-place in . . . a home with an elevator; (2) a home with an in-law suite for my parents . . . my parents were not onboard; they did not want to move—but at least they'd have a place to live if they changed their minds down the road; (3) a home with four fireplaces . . . two back to back fireplaces serving four rooms—upstairs and downstairs; and (4) a home with a heated driveway . . . a "must-have" for my husband—neither one of us had ever lived in a four-season setting before. He'd also made it clear that he would not be snowplowing any driveway ever. And the Lake House from Rosenberger's gallery would be ground zero.

In my mind, this was happening! We'd already purchased our land upfront. And now, we were building a Rosenberger custom home thereon!

Santana Row

Meanwhile, we'd need to sell our current home in order to finance the build. Our home was not a traditional home. We lived in Santana Row. Santana Row is a residential, shopping, dining, and entertainment district built around a main street located 50-miles south of San Francisco. At build out, this Richard Heapes designed project covered an 18-block area and encompassed 680,000 square feet of restaurants, retail space, and commercial office space, 1,201 dwelling units (lofts, flats, townhomes, and villas), luxury Hotel Valencia, salons and spas, movie theaters (CineArts Century Theaters), art galleries (BluFine Art), nightlife, and seven parks. The size and scope of Santana Row made it one of the nation's largest mixed-use projects constructed by a single developer.

Restaurants include: Amber India, Ben & Jerry's, Blowfish Sushi, Chili's Grill & Bar, Cielo, Citrus (Hotel Valencia), Cocola desserts, Consuelo Mexican Bistro, the Counter Burger Bar, Fogo de Chao (Brazilian steakhouse), Lara's Cupcakes, LB Steak, Left Bank Brasserie, Maggiano's Little Italy, Olin Avenue Market, Pasta Pomodoro, Peet's Coffee, Pinkberry, Pizza Antica, Pluto's salads, Pressed Juicery, Rosie McCann's Irish Pub & Restaurant, Roux Louisiana Kitchen, Sino Restaurant & Lounge, Starbucks, Straits Restaurant, Subway, V-Bar Lounge (Hotel Valencia), Veggie Grill, Village California Bistro & Wine Bar, Vintage Wine Bar, Vintage Wine Merchants, Wahoo's Fish Taco, Yankee Pier, the Yard House, and others.

Retail spaces include: Anthropologie, BCBG Max Azria, Best Buy, Blue Jeans Bar, Borders Books and Music, Brooks Brothers, Burberry, Chico's, Cohiba Cigar Lounge, Container Store, Crate & Barrel, Diesel, Donald J. Pliner, Free People, Foot Candy, Gucci, H&M, Kate Spade, Kendra Scott, Loft, Oakley, Orvis, Paper Source, Salvatore Ferragamo, Scotch & Soda, Sephora, Spence Diamonds, St. Croix, St. John Boutique, Sur La Table, Talbots, Ted Baker, Tesla Motors, Tommy Bahamas, Tourneau, Touleh Pet Boutique, Urban Outfitters, Warby Parker, Z Gallerie, and many more.

Salons and spas include: Aveda Atelier Lifestyle Salon Spa, Atelier Studio, Ayoma LifeSpa (Hotel Valencia), Bellarmine Salon, Burke Williams Day Spa, Club One Fitness, Dry Bar, InSpa, Lavande Nail Spa, Morphosis Rejuvenation Studio, and W's Salon.

Santana Row's small town feel inside the big city offers approximately 984 apartment rentals—located in the Serrano and Santana Heights buildings—and 217 units individually owned located in the De Forest, Margo, and Villa Cornet buildings: Villa Cornet with only 21 luxury townhouses, Margo with 100 luxury one-, two-, and three-bedroom loft-style condominiums, and De Forest with 98 luxury multi-level loft homes. All units overlook the pedestrian friendly streets of Santana Row.

My husband and I—previously tenants at both the Margo and Santana Heights properties before units were available for sale—had purchased our loft in the De Forest building in July 2007; a couple of months following the covenant that I had made with God—again, more about this later. (You can also read my memoir, The Secrets of Prayer: When Death Knocked at My Door.)

At the time of purchase, our loft was 1,204 square feet. Then, before we moved in, we did a remodel, which added an additional 150 square feet for a total of 1,354 square feet. It also had a 400 square foot rooftop terrace that sat above Straits Restaurant.

And so it began . . . I started purging and downsizing our belongings. My motto: if I didn't "love, love, love" something, I either gave it away or tossed it. In hindsight, I did get rid of a bit, too much. I wasn't thinking ahead about the unintended consequences of building such a large home: not only would I need to fill it but it would actually be a home large enough that I could celebrate and entertain in, which required additional stuff.

I also purchased moving boxes and tape, and started packing things I knew I wouldn't need for the next couple of years. I even started shopping for the new home I was designing. Of course, anything I purchased would be immediately packed away in boxes, unknowingly to my husband. It would be like Christmas, when I'd unpack.

Next, on to the bigger stuff: I had the oversized sliding glass doors, leading out to the terrace, wheels replaced. I changed the Den closet that I had turned into a built-in bookcase back to a closet. I ripped out my vegetable garden and planted flowers. I gave away my five oversized "pallet" wall planters I had built—each six foot tall by three feet wide by six inches deep—to my neighbor; each one on wheels, so we just rolled them down the hall. I gave away a few more four tiered planters that I had also built to another neighbor, next door; the rest of them I broke down and tossed. Slowly but surely, I'd started staging our home in preparation for sale.

Fortunately, I have a husband who really doesn't pay much attention to his surroundings. He never seems to question me; he was used to me designing and remodeling the homes we've lived in over the years. Instead, our saying was and is "happy spouse, happy life." He's the Chief Financial Officer and I am the Chief Family Officer. His role is breadwinner. I, conversely, am responsible for everything else; I might not bring home a paycheck but he always acknowledges the fact that I work harder than anyone he has ever met.

Consequently, as the house was becoming more and more minimalistic, the boxes were piling up; still, he didn't think anything of it. In fact, in his mind, he still thought any kind of move would be at least two or three years out . . .

Lake City

Nine months later . . . our next visit to Coeur d'Alene would be a mixture: part business, part pleasure. We'd arrive first, visiting showrooms: door, cabinet, and bath hardware outlets; fireplace and masonry shops; flooring and tile stores; granite and countertop display businesses; and home automation equipment and services facilities.

A couple of days later, we'd have dinner with Dan and Joleen, our future neighbors up at The Ridge at Cougar Bay.

The following day, our friends, Scott and Susan—also from California—would join us for the fourth of July weekend holiday and to see what all the fuss was about. When we told them we were moving to Coeur d'Alene, Idaho, they thought we were nuts. They couldn't understand what our draw was to Idaho . . . until they arrived . . .

Northern Panhandle

Coeur d'Alene is beautiful! It's the largest city in Kootenai County, Idaho and in the northern Idaho Panhandle. Coeur d'Alene, Idaho, lies to the north of Lake Coeur d'Alene and is also known as the Lake City. The city is located near two prominent ski resorts, Silver Mountain Resort to the east and Schweitzer Mountain Ski Resort to the north.

Coeur d'Alene is also the home of the Coeur d'Alene Resort Golf course's famous 14th Hole, The Floating Green, which is recognized around the globe as an iconic feat of engineering and design—it's a movable island golf green, 22,000-ton marvel that changes position three times a day via an intricate, underwater cable system.

Annual events include:

- Ironman Coeur d'Alene—a 2.4 mile swim, 112 mile bike and 26.2 mile run in succession—held each August.

- Car d'Lane Classic Car Show held on Father's Day weekend.

- Fourth of July festival starts off with an afternoon parade, concerts in the park, and other activities—the grand finale is a spectacular fireworks display over the lake; held first weekend of July.

- Art on the Green is a three-day celebration of the Arts on the North Idaho College campus—complete with hundreds of booths, children's hands-on art projects, famous ears of corn, and "clothes line" art collections by local artists.

- At the same time, Taste of the Coeur d'Alenes' in the lakeside city park offers food vendors and crafts, along with a seven-block "Downtown Street Fair" in Coeur d'Alene, making for a full weekend of shopping and sightseeing.

- Holiday Light Show beginning thanksgiving weekend, the Coeur d'Alene Resort turns up the bright lights with its Holiday Light Show.

- Throughout the holiday season you can experience America's largest floating holiday light show and laser extravaganza. Cruise boats take you on Lake Coeur d'Alene to view the animated light displays and holiday scenes along the Coeur d'Alene Resort shoreline, and then a special visit to Santa's workshop.

- Other events include breakfasts with Santa, Sunday brunches with Dickens Carolers and Mrs. Clause, Santa Cruises for the very young, a downtown Christmas tree lighting ceremony, fireworks shows and a lighted parade.

Instead of staying at the Coeur d'Alene Resort, this time we used our Starwood points and stayed at the Marriott Hotel. We figured with all the fourth of July festivities going on that weekend, downtown would be overcrowded, and too cumbersome to get around in; besides, we had a rental car and more commitments to meet bankers and our builder again after the holiday. Scott and Susan also stayed at the Marriott and had their own rental car.

Together, we took them to see our property and then showed them around downtown. They couldn't believe not only the beauty of it all but also how much there was to do—they loved outdoor activities: arts and wine festivals, farmers markets, golfing, hiking, ziplining, paddle boarding, skiing, you name it.

We even took them just outside of town to the city of Sandpoint in Bonner County for lunch; another fabulous town just 45-minutes up the road—halfway between Coeur d'Alene and the Canadian border. They, too, saw the attraction Coeur d'Alene had to offer.

Small Town Feel

Scott and Susan are some of our very best friends, and they also were looking to get out of California—albeit for different reasons. We all agreed, that the Coeur d'Alene lifestyle was much like the one we were very familiar with in California, but better: lots of taverns, restaurants, music and entertainment, shopping, museums, parks, and much more—but a lot less people, crime was minimal, and chain businesses were excluded from the downtown area. The city of Coeur d'Alene catered to the locals and small town feel.

But it would be the reasonable cost of living in the city of Coeur d'Alene that would appeal to them the most. Nonetheless, they had other places they wanted to explore as well before making any life changing decisions.

We wrapped up our weekend together, early evening, on the fourth of July, when we took up residence on the green in front of the Coeur d'Alene Resort to watch the fireworks.

But it would be the aftermath, immediately following the event, which would put us all in a tailspin. Apparently, they had blocked off all of the surrounding streets around downtown, four streets deep. Not only was I completely unfamiliar with the city, I was also the designated driver!

Nonetheless, thankfully—unlike California drivers—people in Coeur d'Alene are very courteous drivers—another plus! Traffic was backed up, bumper to bumper, everywhere. Ultimately, to get back to our hotel, on a whim, I purposely went down a blocked off street—

something that shocked all of my passengers; I always followed the rules.

Even so, they were also very pleased; the guys needed to use the urinal stat!

The end of the street led me to three lanes of traffic ahead. As I crossed the first two lanes, I ended up cutting someone off—again, cars were bumper to bumper—to get across into the third lane to turn down yet another side street.

Finally, I got us all back to the Marriott safely. There were no horns, no gestures, no speeding up; instead, I was graciously let in to an otherwise untenable situation.

Wow! You've got to love this place! Thank you, Lord Jesus Christ, for introducing us to Coeur d'Alene and giving us an opportunity to be part of this incredibly blessed city!

Banker Meetings

The next day, Scott and Susan had left, and it was just my husband and I, again. Our next order of business was to meet with bankers. If we were going to build a home at The Ridge, we were going to need financing. Along the way, we learned: a home construction loan is a short-term, higher-interest loan that provides the funds required to build a residential property. Thereafter, the construction loan is converted into a term loan, also called a mortgage, in which the home is used as collateral.

Inasmuch, as part of my pre-trip planning, I had contacted each of the four bankers that were listed on the Rosenberger Construction website and had scheduled appointments with all four.

One by one, as we began interviewing bankers, we found out that different banks did different things. After our third meeting: we had one banker that only provided construction loans, another banker that only provided term loans, and the last banker we interviewed provided both construction and term loans. The latter banker made the most sense—one stop shopping.

So before meeting with the fourth banker, I called him and inquired as to what type of loans he offers; again, only construction loans so we canceled that appointment. When the time came to move forward on the financing phase, we'd go with the banker that provided both construction and term loans.

Builder Meeting

Next, we were to meet with our builder for the second time. I had finally convinced my husband that moving to Idaho was becoming a reality. I explained that we needed the builder to walk the property for two reasons: (1) to determine how buildable our site was, and (2) to confirm that the 5,000 square foot home that I was designing would fit on the lot. In addition, since we had also found out that Rosenberger Construction had his own in-house architect on staff—going outside to any third-party would not be necessary nor cost effective—we'd bring a $5,000 check so that I could start working with his architect on elevations and preliminary drawings.

Our meeting with Ron Rosenberger started in his office. As I began to bring him up to speed—on what I had been up to—it wasn't hard for me to notice that he really wasn't interested in all the PowerPoint slides I had brought; about 90 pages. Albeit, he was most gracious; instead, we discussed the basics: the size of the home, how many bedrooms and bathrooms, and how much it'd cost to build a custom 5,000 square foot home.

Afterward, my husband and I, were pleasantly surprised to learn that building our custom home could be done at a relatively reasonable price: homes built from 2000 to 2017 average price per square foot was $164; so our 5,000 square foot home multiplied by $164 in 2017 would cost approximately $820,000. This was something we could afford if we sold our existing home. Then, to my surprise, he asked for my slides after all and told me he would forward them to his architect.

Next, Ron introduced us to his wife, Shelley; from their website: A Coeur d'Alene native, Shelley's first career in education spanned 22-years as an elementary school teacher and administrator in Lakeland and Coeur d'Alene public schools. She joined forces with the Rosenberger team formally in 2004 and serves as the office manager and project coordinator. Her experience working with teams means you have both a coach and cheerleader on your project from the start to insure your new home is everything you dreamed of . . .

Shelley would be my point person going forward and she would also join us the next day, at our scheduled meeting with The Ridge at Cougar Bay's Homeowners Association. All home site owners were required to attend an orientation meeting prior to submitting house plans for approval. We'd explain that we lived out of state, and wanted Shelley to be the point person on our project. Ron then concluded the meeting, telling us he would meet us up at our lot for the off-site portion of our meeting . . .

Builder Site Meeting

Eric and I were the first to arrive at our lot. Upon our arrival, we were happy to see our future neighbor, Dan: he was working outside in his yard. We had just had dinner with him and his wife, Joleen, a few nights before. Dan was also the President of the Homeowners Association at The Ridge and our point person as to the history of our lot. So we briefed him on our meeting with Ron and told him we thought we would be neighbors within the next 18-months. Again, this timeframe—our plan; our builder's plan—would not be in harmony with God's plan; God's perfect timing . . .

A few minutes later, Ron arrived and assessed our lot. He told us it was a very buildable lot and that there should be no problem building a 5,000 square foot home on the site. He also mentioned that he was very familiar with The Ridge's Design Review Guidelines since he was one of the builders up at The Ridge. I don't know why . . . but neither my husband nor I bothered to ask, which other home(s) at The Ridge had he built? Call it ignorance or just plain overwhelmed, we both stayed silent. Of course, looking back, we should have asked—it would have been the right thing to do, the right thing to show a little interest in his work. Nevertheless, he was unassuming as always.

Then . . . it happened again . . .

As Ron wrapped up our meeting, he casually said something that didn't make any sense to either of us at the time. He pointed to a home, two lots over and said, "Now that's a nice house."

It was the same house—the first house we saw—sitting at the top of the hill, the day we found and purchased our lot.

Again, like a couple of oblivious disinterested people—under normal circumstance we are both very humble people—we just stood there in silence.

Much later, we'd learn, he had built that house in 2009.

Looking back; at the time, I guess since we were building a home, we weren't really interested in looking at homes. Plus the fact that The Ridge required each home to be unique; I didn't want to accidentally copy another home and get rejected by the Homeowners Association. Likewise, we thought it was insignificant to see what the neighbors might have built.

Ron closed the meeting, telling us his architect would get back to us with preliminary drawings. Now this comment woke me up!

So I asked, "how long before I should expect something?"

His response, "a few weeks."

That sounded like a long time.

So I asked, "how long would it take to build the 5,000 square foot home?"

He said, about six to nine months once they broke ground.

Homeowners Association Meeting

The next day, Shelley met us at The Ridge's Homeowners Association office for our orientation meeting. Shelley explained she was very familiar with The Ridge's Design Review Guidelines. The HOA representatives then told us that upon submitting house plans for review and approval, they would require a $10,000 deposit prior to the build. This would ensure that homeowners followed the Design Review Guidelines. If there were no issues after the build, the HOA would refund the money. Immediately, I countered back; I told the HOA representative that I knew they had a bond program where we would only have to put up ten percent or $1,000 instead of the $10,000.

Thank you Joleen, our future neighbor, for this information a few nights before.

The HOA representative seemed a bit annoyed about my knowledge, but reluctantly conceded.

At the close of this meeting, I handed Shelley a $5,000 check to begin working with Rosenberger's architect.

Trials and Triumphs

Back in California . . . I realized things were not going so well. My anxiety was creeping back and getting the best of me again. In addition to running my own household, I had gone from raising my kids to full-time caregiver to both my aging parents—spending 30- to 40-hours a week at their home. Changing beds, doing laundry, grocery shopping, more shopping, and what seemed to be a merry-go-round of never ending doctor's appointments and pharmacy visits, there didn't seem to be enough of me to go around anymore. It was all getting to be too much!

At one point, both my parents would be in wheelchairs. Dad's dementia made it difficult for him to walk; he used a transport chair. Then, mom was diagnosed with diabetic Charcot foot—her bones in her foot shattered—so she had to stay off her foot for eight weeks, also in a wheelchair; she claimed the scooters to get her around were too hard on her bad knee.

As a result of my parent's increasing difficulties, my mom was finally considering the idea of moving to Idaho and living with us. She was beginning to realize that her and dad's caregiving needs would likely increase going forward.

Consequently, she was also becoming—more and more—involved in designing the in-law suite I'd planned. But nothing I designed seemed good enough—she always wanted more. In fact, my mom wanted a one-bedroom apartment for her and dad in our home—a house inside of a house! And in her mind, square footage should have been unlimited. I blamed HGTV; she was a big fan and told me she'd seen it done all the time.

Aging Parents

My parents were becoming increasingly, more and more unhappy. They felt like we were abandoning them. My husband and I were the only family left in California besides my dad's brother and his wife, their daughter and her family. But they didn't have any intentions of ever leaving their home; they had been in their home 50-plus years.

Until . . . my father's fall . . .

While trying to help my mom, my father had forgotten his cane, and fell off the cement step leading out to the back hardscape patio. Mom had to call 911 and then us. When my husband and I arrived at the hospital, we learned that my father had cracked his head open and broken two ribs—but he'd be fine.

For years, we had nicknamed him the "come back king"—because whenever you'd think he might be at the end of his rope, he'd always bounce back.

Nevertheless, he was in bad shape and mom didn't want to leave him alone. This incident felt all too familiar; history was repeating itself again:

The Bible says, "The thing that has been, it is that which will be; and that which is done is that which will be done: and there is no new thing under the sun" (Ecclesiastes 1:9).

My husband's three parents may have successively passed away relieving me of any more caregiving duties, but now I had assumed the ever-increasing role as caregiver to my own parents. Apparently, I had an innate responsibility to help loved ones as they aged, but were there limits?

For years, my father would drive over to Santana Row—where I was living at the time—with his dog, Molly; and we would take morning walks around the beautiful streets of Santana Row. Then, after he had to give up his driver's license—he couldn't pass his driving test anymore; he was diagnosed with early onset dementia. I'd pick him and Molly up—with walker in tow—and drive us back to Santana Row for our morning walks; this also gave my mom time to sleep in during the weekdays. Upon our return, mom would make us breakfast.

But now, after my dad's fall, my caregiving services would become more like a 9:00 a.m. to 5:00 p.m. job, Monday through Thursday . . .

Lockout

At home, I carried on . . . I continued deep cleaning, packing, and staging our loft, and the boxes were piling up: all the boxes were the same size, I had most of them staged in the Den, and I'd even made strategic paths for someone to be able to walk around the box piles and still be able to see the area.

Next, I was anticipating the required home inspection prior to a sale: smoke detectors, plug-in carbon monoxide detectors, and any electrical, plumbing, or HVAC issues. All the while . . . deep inside . . . I knew I was falling apart . . .

Then the final straw . . .

I had the air conditioner guy come out to replace the filter in our unit above the entryway. The downstairs building main entrance door wasn't working with the card key; so I'd have to go back and forth, letting him in and out.

But, of course, when we left together to go downstairs to retrieve a filter from his van, the front door closed and we were locked out— the dog, my cell phone, and my house keys were all inside.

Nonetheless, I held it together a little while longer and retrieved the filter; I told the guy I would replace it myself. He felt bad and kindly told me to call him if I had any trouble.

Next, I went back upstairs and knocked on our neighbor's door. As soon as Barbara opened the door—I couldn't contain myself any longer—I burst into tears. I was losing it!

I explained, "I accidently locked myself out of our apartment. Can I please borrow your phone to call Eric?"

She agreed.

I called him, and not surprisingly, he wants to argue with me. He is not listening. He thinks it is my neighbor calling him at work on accident; he's trying to tell her to call me.

Still sobbing, I cried, "No! It's me; I got locked out of our loft."

As always, he turns into prince charming, telling me he's on his way home. After I hung up, Barbara offered me a glass of wine, which I gladly accepted.

While we waited for my husband, I calmed down a bit, and we started to catch up. As I was updating her on what I was doing in our unit, she stopped me in mid-sentence . . .

She said, "You can't sell a house with all those boxes staged in the house."

It had not dawned on me before, but she was right. Now I was a smart woman, why couldn't I see this?

As I pondered my question in silence for a moment: I realized, I was in a rut, just going through the motions. I wasn't paying attention. I wasn't paying attention to God! I was so caught up in my so-called "obligations," I wasn't thinking clearly—putting God first:

The Bible says, "In all your ways acknowledge Him, and He will direct your paths" (Proverbs 3:6).

I was in over my head caring for my parents full-time four days a week . . . God was moving me to Idaho with or without my parents; it would be their choice, I wasn't abandoning them. My parents could afford full-time help if they sold their home and moved.

I was in over my head designing my dream home—something I had never done before—a house inside of a house, to boot; this did not appeal to me at all! I was paying more attention to what my mom wanted than God's plan . . . God was moving me to Idaho but would I really be building a house inside of a house?

I was in over my head with clutter; I had cluttered my home with moving boxes. But I hated clutter; it drove me crazy! I never felt good unless my house was in order; only then could I move on to other things . . . God was moving me to Idaho so that I could "move on to other things" and make good on my covenant I'd made with him back in 2007: God's calling, my mission—a single moment in time that changed my life.

Again, you can read more about this in my memoir, The Secrets of Prayer: When Death Knocked at My Door.

There it was . . . my parents, my dream home, and my boxes . . . this was why I had returned to a state of anxiety, restlessness, and was downright miserable all over again. Of course, I was hitting the wall! God was trying to get my attention! He used my front door closing and lockout to get me to Barbara. And now, He was using Barbara to get me back on track . . . well, with at least one of the three reasons my anxiety had returned . . . my boxes; I needed my house in order to clear the path for bigger things to come . . .

As I came out of my mental deliberation, I asked Barbara, but where would I find a storage unit close by that I could trust?

Once more, crime was at an all-time high in California, they kept the jails full, and didn't even bother coming out to investigate: rape, burglary, car theft, and so on, anymore.

She didn't hesitate. She told me, her and her husband had one down the road—they used it for their business—a couple of miles away. She assured me they hadn't had any problems and it had been five years.

Finally, I had hope again! I was re-energized!

But for not getting locked out of the house and having this conversation with my neighbor, Barbara, I wouldn't have realized I was on the wrong path! I wouldn't have realized that my boxes piling up in the loft were contributing to my stress level. I wouldn't have realized that I needed to move my boxes out of the loft before I could sell it. Now, with this "ah ha" moment, I'd immediately adjust my course, and move the boxes into a local storage unit.

Shortly after my husband got home and rescued me, he thought he was going to sit down and play video games since he left work early. But I had other plans. I told him about my conversation with Barbara. Then, I explained, storage units were in high demand; so we needed to move fast.

Sure enough, after we arrived at the storage facility, they only had two units available: a very small unit that would never work and a larger one. The larger one was an inside unit that opened to a short-walkway to where you'd park to load and unload. It was perfect. We rented it on the spot. Thank you, Jesus!

Apartment Hunting

In just a couple of months, the building maintenance guys and I had the storage unit filled: 120 medium sized boxes, 31-piece Lovesac sectional, and all the terrace furniture. Suddenly, I had at least one area in my life that gave me a sense of calm again. The house, too, was coming along and it was starting to look more like a staged home, which also pleased me.

But since we were selling, we'd need another place to stay while our home was being built. So I decided to delegate this task to my husband. In my mind, this fell under his Chief Financial Officer role! If it had to do with money, he'd have to handle it. His parameters would be: downtown Sunnyvale—in the city where we met—lots of bars and restaurants, music and entertainment, and shopping downstairs from the apartments above and surrounding area. The apartment also had to have in-unit laundry and be dog friendly.

My husband didn't disappoint. He found the perfect apartment complex; it met all my requirements. However, it was also the only apartment complex that filled my criteria . . . we'd need to move fast.

The next day, I was having dental surgery on both sides of my lower jaw—I was finally addressing a 20-something mistake, I'd made 30-something years prior; it was cheaper to pull a couple of teeth than get crowns. Nonetheless, immediately after surgery, I told my husband I wanted to head over to the apartment building he found—I was feeling that sense of urgency again. My husband was concerned; and asked if I really wanted to see the apartment that day. Without hesitation, I told him a resounding yes!

When we arrived downtown, miraculously we found a parking spot right away! Finding parking downtown was always a problem.

We then walked a short block to the Solstice apartment homes and introduced ourselves to the rental agent inside; we explained we were looking for a one-bedroom apartment. He informed us; he had only one unit available—it was a one-bedroom unit. So I asked if we could see it? He then showed us a unit on the third-floor that overlooked the pool and recreation area; it was perfect!

Now my husband was experiencing some anxiety of his own. He was worried about paying rent and a mortgage at the same time. So in an effort to give him some time to adjust, I turned to the rental agent. I asked if we could get pre-approved and put a deposit down to hold the unit for 24 hours? The agent agreed.

Then . . . no sooner had we completed the paperwork and wrote a check for the deposit . . . another couple walked in looking for a one-bedroom unit. The agent explained, we'd just put a deposit down on the only unit he had available—but that they could be placed on a waiting list . . .

Talk about timing! God is good! God is very, very good! We were obviously following God's plan. And the more we followed God's plan, all the more blessings followed!

Listing Our Loft

On our way home . . . I wasted no time . . . I called our friends, Susie and Jurgen, who were also realtors that just happened to live three doors down from us. Susie was out of town, but Jurgen was available and agreed to meet with us that evening. In addition to being our friends, living and working in Santana Row, they were the go-to realtors for the property. In fact, they had just closed on a unit at the end of our hallway—following a frenzy of interest.

That night, when Jurgen arrived, I was very thankful that he got to see our loft looking more like a staged house; no more boxes, they were all in storage. Although he had been in our unit once before for a book launch after-party in 2011, he didn't really remember the interior. So I began . . . prior to moving in, we did a remodel . . .

Upstairs: (1) closed in open space above kitchen—giving the primary bedroom a sitting area, which added 150 square feet, (2) added granite tops to the loft half walls at the top of the staircase, (3) installed mirror back, glass shelves, and granite top to bedroom nook, (4) boxed in upstairs exposed 30-foot long industrial HVAC tube and placed dropdown lighting therefrom, (5) installed glass shower door in the primary bathroom, (6) replaced double vanity mirrors with a single wall to wall vanity mirror in primary bathroom, (7) replaced primary bathroom lighting, (8) repurposed downstairs bathroom upper cabinet above toilet in upstairs primary bathroom, and (9) added chandeliers in primary bathroom and primary walk-in closet.

Downstairs: (1) eliminated small entry closet—opening space up— replaced with wall unit coatrack and cubby configuration, (2) replaced Den half wall with glass wall and hardware, (3) eliminated Den closet curtain-door and added open-closet system, (4) painted kitchen cabinets, and (5) stained kitchen and half bath cement floors.

In addition, installed carpet (1,250 square feet) on both floors and painted interior; accent walls, included: headboard wall, two 22-foot high walls running on either side of the downstairs sliding glass doors and upstairs windows, lower level Den ceiling, and exposed industrial HVAC system in the Den.

After we toured the loft, we went over the numbers. Jurgen had brought over comps and had a number of what he thought we should list our unit at. This didn't mesh with our number. Our number took into consideration the remodel and added square footage.

Our building had 98 units and our unit was unique; there was only one other unit that looked similar but it didn't have the large rooftop terrace.

After further discussion and some additional negotiation, the three of us agreed to list our loft at $1,025,000. But we weren't done yet . . .

Still, my husband was worried about carrying a mortgage and paying rent for an apartment at the same time. We discussed his concerns. Then Jurgen made a statement that I thought was strange: he "assured us" that our unit would sell in less than 60-days.

Assurance? Does he have a crystal ball? Did he know something we didn't know?

Nonetheless, this was good news; so we stayed silent (apparently, we do this a lot) and signed the listing paperwork.

Later that night, I'd call and send an email to the rental office at Solstice; telling them we would take the apartment.

Moving On

The next day, we signed an eleven-month lease and immediately took possession of the apartment.

There it was again, another peculiar thing: why an eleven-month lease? Why not a standard twelve-month lease? But, of course, we didn't question it.

Susie had referred us to some local movers. I called them and they just happened to be available during our timeframe—thank you God! So we hired them on the spot to do two moves: (1) move our furniture and belongings to the apartment in Sunnyvale, and (2) move my 31 fruit and nut trees—all self-contained in oversized pots on wheels—from our terrace in the sky to my parent's backyard in the city of Campbell.

My mom, reluctantly, agreed to let me store my trees at her house until we moved to Idaho.

Gardening always had a very calming effect on me; hence, in addition to the trees, there were my previously purged wall garden planters, three arbors, four-tier planters, and vegetable garden—I was also very big on nutrition and a self-sustaining lifestyle.

In the meantime, I'd also need to work with the state department of Idaho's agriculture people to see if I could even bring my trees with us. Then, if I had the okay to do so, I'd still need to try to find a moving company that would be willing to transport them to Idaho.

Back in downtown Sunnyvale, we quickly returned to our old habits; this was our old stomping grounds and the home of one of our favorite watering holes. I told my husband, I thought it would be fitting to close our last chapter in California—in the city where we met—before beginning a new chapter in Idaho.

Surprise, surprise. Many of our old friends were still there and a new adventure began . . . I immediately reconnected with my lifelong girlfriend, Maria. She'd introduce us to many new friends—some, too, would become lasting friendships as well. In particular, Pat and Ditra, who'd we eventually hire for a short stent in Idaho—more about this later. Maria was married to Steve; and I didn't know it at the time, but later, God would use them to ignite a fire deep inside of me— answering my question: What am I supposed to be doing? How was I going to fulfill that promise I had made with God ten years ago?

Meanwhile, I couldn't stop thinking about what Jurgen had said. Was he right? Would our loft sell in less than 60-days? If so, when would we move to Idaho? When would we see preliminary drawings from the architect? Did my dream home really include building a house inside of a house for my parents? How was I going to make good on my promise to God?

Then . . . as my ramblings continued in my head. Suddenly, God the Holy Spirit, came upon me and brought a strong sense of peace over me (always accompanied by chills); this was more than ever before. I didn't need to have any of these answers. God would answer them . . . one by one . . . each in his perfect timing. My only job was to have faith . . . live a life that was others-centered and a life that put God first . . . in return, I'd receive His blessings . . .

Blessings Abundant

Susie and Jurgen were truly a blessing. They took care of everything: They had our loft professionally cleaned, the windows cleaned, the carpets cleaned, the terrace power washed, planted more flowers in the oversized terrace planters, and much more. Then they arranged for our loft to be professionally staged. (We'd pay this fee upfront.) They brought in professional photographers as part of their marketing plan. They even took care of a couple of minor points that the home inspection report called out. Then, they had an open house.

And, just like Jurgen assured us it would happen, "our unit would sell in less than 60-days." It sold in just 11-days! We received a full ask cash offer! Maybe he did have a crystal ball . . . maybe the buyer who lost out on the sale of the unit down the hall . . . or, maybe it was just simply, God's perfect timing . . .

In the end, it didn't matter "how" it happened. What mattered is that it did happen; our loft sold, and now we would have the funds to finance our home in Coeur d'Alene. This was truly just another blessing—one of so many—all designed by God! It all was validation that we were on the right path! Our Lord God was leading us down a path that would move us out of California to Idaho.

But more importantly, He was clearing a path for me to fulfill my promise to Him; that covenant I had made with Him ten years earlier.

In 2007, when death knocked at my door, I promised God: I'll do anything you want me to do—if you, please, let me live to finish raising my young sons. Well, I'm still alive today and my sons are long grown. And now, He was preparing me to make good on my part of our arrangement. I was ready; I meant what I promised—but I still didn't have clarity on what God wanted me to do. What would my calling be? I guess, I'd find out in His perfect timing . . .

Builder Bids

After several months, working back and forth on preliminary drawings with the architect; we finally received the numbers—Bid Set—of what it would cost to build our home, which had now grown to a 6,000 square foot home: $2.3 million! Way out of our league! This was nearly three times more than we originally budgeted for; this would put the house at $383 per square foot. I was crushed! I wanted to cry!

I called the builder—Rosenberger Construction—immediately and Ron explained: Coeur d'Alene was experiencing a building boom, labor was in short supply, and materials had skyrocketed. But my biggest issue, he said, my costs doubled when we started building a house inside of a house for my parents.

My mother wanted a full kitchen—large enough for the 40-inch round dining room table she'd recently purchased; in her mind a kitchenette was not an option—but this made no sense, she no longer liked to cook. She really didn't want to downsize. Instead, in addition to the eat-in kitchen, she also wanted a living room, bedroom, handicap bathroom, walk-in closet, and a washer and dryer setup. She was trying to move her 1,400 square foot home into an in-law suite in our home.

I'm a people pleaser—to a point—especially when it comes to my parents. So I decided it was time for me to bite the bullet and break the bad news to my mom. Afterwards, she said, she would downsize but a kitchen would not be off the table. She couldn't understand how a 6,000 square foot home couldn't accommodate her wants. (I was getting nowhere.) But she really wasn't the problem. I was the problem. She might have been acting unreasonable, but I was letting her get away with it . . .

I called Ron back and we strategized a bit. But, he too, was frustrated. We'd been in "architect design mode" for nearly five months now and neither one of us really wanted to start over. Nevertheless, he said, he would see what he could do on costs—but that I needed to tell him what I could take off the table, too.

After that last phone call, I felt like my dream home was slipping away. But was it really my dream home . . . after all . . . building a house inside of a house?

I tried to work with my mother to no avail. Her bigger issue was that she didn't want to move. With my free services as caregiver, my parents could still afford to live in their home. She was a bit angry, too, that I was moving which might force her to have to move anyway. My husband and I, and my dad's brother and his wife and their family, were the only relatives they had still living in California. My three brothers, their seven kids, and eleven grandchildren all lived—in close proximity to one another—in Florida. But my parents hated the weather in Florida; so in their mind, Florida was out of the question . . .

Well, I did my part; I tried to downsize the house to the best of my ability and forwarded my revisions to Ron. He then did his part; he had his people (his son) rework the numbers and once again got back to us: $1.78 million! And with his backlog, our home wouldn't be ready for another couple of years!

Now, I was extremely irritated! When I compared the Bid Set, it seemed that all of the savings ($520,000) came out of the Allowance section. This meant, even if we went to contract, we'd quickly run the tab back up to $2.3 million to cover the deflated Allowance amounts.

Although, with the recent windfall we'd just received the prior month . . . another blessing. Thank you, Uncle Jimmy and Gilead! But for Gilead issuing a stock dividend program and mailing checks to Marin County's probate court, we would never had discovered Marin County's blunder. Then the ensuing second probate would take nearly two more years before final payout. As a result—once again, in God's perfect timing—we could actually afford Rosenberger's price, either way. But that wasn't the point!

Nonetheless, I'd face the music and call the builder back again. I apologized and told him we would need to start over. Our new budget would be at $1.2 million firm and we'd be cooperative with whatever he came up with. He then told me, we had more than exhausted our original $5,000 towards architect drawings and he'd need an additional $7,000 to start the process over. We agreed and mailed him a check.

In the meantime, I'd book another trip to Idaho to start working with the banker we selected. We wanted to have all of our ducks in a row, so that we could go to contract as soon as the next set of house plans were finalized.

Winter Wonderland

Back in Idaho . . . this would be a short trip. It was mid-January and we'd get to see the snow there for the first time. It was beautiful! It felt like a winter wonderland! Nothing like the winters in Lake Tahoe, Nevada, which both my husband and I had experienced in our earlier years—before we met. In Coeur d'Alene, the summers are short, warm, dry, and mostly clear, and the winters can be very cold and long. Still, chains and studded snow tires weren't necessary; simply any kind of four-wheel drive or all-wheel drive or having all weather tires would usually suffice. This was good to know.

We didn't rent a car this time, but we did stay at the Marriott hotel again. The Marriott backed up to the Riverstone Village: Riverstone is an open-air lifestyle-shopping destination with condominiums, hotels, shopping, restaurants, coffee shops, a movie theater, and much more. Strolling along the cobblestone streets as you shopped, dined, and played, felt much like being back in Santana Row or downtown Sunnyvale. We'd be in and out of our hotel over the next three days.

Hands down, best of all was downtown Coeur d'Alene. It felt like home. We'd now been downtown enough times that we'd met several of the bartenders and locals. We'd start there . . . the next day we'd meet with the banker to get pre-qualified for both the upcoming construction loan and then the conversion term loan. Following this meeting, we treated ourselves to lunch at the Floating Green Restaurant—watching the golfers boat back and forth between the landlocked golf course and the famous 14th Hole, Floating Green. We ended our trip with dinner at Anthony's restaurant. Anthony's at Coeur d'Alene is located in the Riverstone community and features its own scenic waterfront setting—it has two outdoor-fireplaces, and yet, another stunning view . . .

House on the Hill at The Ridge

Back in California . . . a week later . . . still, nothing new from the builder. I was becoming more and more dejected; feeling disheartened and uneasy with what the builder would come up with . . . I needed to do something—but I wanted to give Rosenberger the benefit of the doubt. I'd never built a home before; the whole process was completely unrelated to anything I'd ever done before. So I decided to put my "lawyer hat" back on and do some "due diligence" before we'd decide to go into contract with the builder. I wanted confirmation about the status of Coeur d'Alene's building situation.

So my husband and I called Dan, our neighbor who lived next to our lot. He and his wife had become friends of ours over the last year. In addition to his day job, he also just happened to be a pastor.

Was God speaking to me, again?

On the phone, I explained we were getting discouraged . . . I wanted to know if the builder's "statement of facts" were true or exaggerated? And his "answer" corroborated with what the builder was telling us: Coeur d'Alene was experiencing an incredible housing boom. Building materials were at an all-time high. But the biggest factor was the shortage of laborers, especially framers—carpenters who assemble the major structural elements of a wood-framed home: framers build walls out of studs, sills, and headers; build floors from joists and beams; and frame roofs using ridge poles and rafters. He told us, he'd even seen billboards on the freeway advertising for said day laborers. This didn't make us feel any better but at least we knew now, the "facts were true and verified."

Then . . .

As I paused to regroup my thoughts . . . Dan interrupted.

He said, "Why don't you just buy Bill and Jess' home?"

This stopped us dead in our tracks! We hadn't been looking at homes for sale. Not to mention, early on, when we unintentionally blew off our builder when he made a couple of remarks: he had built another home up at The Ridge; and later on, pointed to that house on top of the hill and said, "now that's a nice house."

We asked Dan, "which home?

And when he answered, chills soared up and down my body! I could hear God loud and clear, now! You are not building a house inside of a house! You are not building a home! Haven't you hit the wall enough? Wake up!

Why hadn't I gotten it before? The signs were always there! God was communicating with me but I was missing his message: I have a home waiting for you . . . I have a home you can afford now . . . I have a home you can move into now . . .

I get chills up and down my spine right now as I am writing this—replaying it in my mind.

It was that home! The home on top of the hill! The first home we saw when we first drove up to The Ridge at Cougar Bay. And it was a Rosenberger home!

This was no coincidence! God divinely orchestrated this! God had held back Rosenberger from closing a deal with us so that we'd find this home.

This home was just two lots over from our lot. Yet, it was on a considerably larger lot, on higher ground, turned to give it tons of privacy, and it had a slightly better view than ours—its view could see more of Lake Coeur d'Alene around the corner. And the couple had just put it back on the market. There it was again; history was repeating itself; I repeat:

> The Bible says, "The thing that has been, it is that which will
> be; and that which is done is that which will be done: and there
> is no new thing under the sun" (Ecclesiastes 1:9).

Our lot, too, had just been put back on the market when we purchased it. Would we purchase this home?

We asked Dan for the real estate agent's name.

Since we didn't have a realtor, we felt it might be beneficial to work with the same realtor the sellers were using.

Then . . . it happened again . . . history repeated itself: Dan explained that this realtor also lived up at The Ridge. Like our friends, Susie and Jurgen—the go-to relators in Santana Row—he, too, was also the go-to realtor up at The Ridge.

We thanked Dan, profusely! We were over the moon!

Due Diligence

We wasted no time, we called the realtor immediately . . . he was intrigued how we found him. He had the home up for sale—off and on—for more than two years. It started at $1.75 million and seemed to be dropping $50,000 every six-months. They were asking $1.5 million. That night, the realtor emailed us his contact information and access to a 3D tour and drone video of the house.

When I opened the email, all of a sudden, I felt a sense of urgency surge in me again. A feeling I'd finally become very familiar with. I was paying attention and I knew this meant something.

Then, I remembered something that I had said to my husband, back in December: I told him, "If I wasn't out of California before the end of the upcoming New Year—eleven months from then—I was going to have a nervous breakdown." The rate things were going with the builder, there was no way we'd be living in Coeur d'Alene before the end of the year.

Then, we played the video . . . again . . . and again . . . and again. We couldn't believe what we were viewing . . . the home looked very similar to our dream home I was designing, but without the house inside of a house—albeit, plenty of room for my parents. It had a daylight basement, oversized four-car garage, bonus room and half bathroom above the garage. It included a new elevator that would be installed in the next few weeks. In 2009, when they built the house, they built-in just the elevator shaft.

Upstairs and downstairs, it had two floor-to-ceiling gas-fireplaces that supported two areas (main floor and lower level great rooms) and surround sound throughout the home as well as outside on the deck.

The lower level had two guest bedrooms between a Jack and Jill bathroom, second primary suite—bedroom, bathroom, and walk-in closet—family room, wet-bar and kitchenette, wine cellar, mechanical room with a large gun safe bolted to the floor, large linen closet, storage closet under the staircase, and large unfinished storage room—this room was huge! Outside, it had a covered patio that was already plumbed for a hot tub.

The main level had the main primary suite—bedroom, bathroom with heated floors and a spa tub, water closet, two linen closets, and walk-in closet, with a glass door opening out to the deck; a large foyer, office, living room, dining room with another glass door opening out to the deck; large kitchen, large breakfast bar, pantry; half bathroom, large laundry room, and mudroom area. The mudroom area had a separate entrance and porch; in other words, the home had two front doors and porches!

Although it did not have a "heated driveway," it had a long curved driveway that led to a large circular private portion—you could park at least a dozen cars on the driveway. And it was 6,087 square feet! This was a dream house! It was beyond perfect!

Why hadn't it sold? If it cost $2.3+ million to re-build this home, plus another $500,000 paid for the lot, why were they only asking $1.5 million? The answer, the housing boom in Coeur d'Alene! In 2009, the cost to build this 6,087 square foot home was $1,250,000 (because of all the upgrades), plus the land brought its total to $1.75 million— selling at this higher price, the couple would have just broken even. The realtor claimed they overpaid for the land; but in actuality, it took them three years to talk the previous owner into selling the lot to them. It's by far the best parcel out of the 77-home-sites up at The Ridge. But, the new cost to build these kinds of larger homes had not caught up with the market. We'd score at $1.5 million!

There was nothing to deliberate, not only was it the best financial solution, the best investment solution; more importantly, it seemed it was God's plan for us to purchase this house! It had been waiting for us all along. Unbeknownst to us, it had been on the market ever since we purchased our lot. This was a neon sign from God!

Closing the Deal

The next evening—after my husband got off work—we called the realtor back and told him we wanted the home. He kind of chuckled and asked, how much?

I can only assume, but I got the distinct impression that he'd probably received many low-ball offers over the last couple of years—it was always the most expensive home listing at The Ridge at Cougar Bay.

We told him, full ask, of course!

This sparked his curiosity.

He then asked, don't you want to come out and see the home first?

We said, no.

He was dumbfounded. He couldn't understand why we'd make an offer at this price point—$1.5 million—on a home we've never visited.

But, once he got it, we were serious buyers; he asked, who was representing us?

We explained, since we hadn't been in the market for a home, we didn't have a realtor. Instead, we wanted to know if he could also represent us?

He thought about it, we discussed his fiduciary duties; we even agreed to sign any "conflict of interest waiver," if necessary. Finally, he agreed to not only represent both the couple and us on this transaction, but he'd also list our lot for sale pending acceptance of our offer.

Offer and Acceptance

The next morning, our realtor would present our offer to the couple. We were excited but a bit nervous, too. If we could see what a great deal this house was, how come no one else did?

Later that morning, we heard from our realtor—our offer was accepted: As part of the offer, we also agreed to let the couple stay in the home for up to three months—rent-free, of course.

We still had that 11-month lease at our apartment. Again, my husband and I have never been greedy people, quite the opposite; the couple was older, both handicapped, and we felt it was the right thing to do.

Timing could not have been more perfect for all parties: (1) Our realtor was on the verge of losing the couple as clients—two and a half years later, the house still wasn't sold. (2) But for our neighbor, Dan, we wouldn't have stumbled upon this home for sale. We never even considered purchasing a home; all along we wrongly thought we were building a home. It had just been re-listed with yet another price reduction just three days earlier before we made our offer. (3) The couple had a trip planned to the east coast—they'd been invited to a wedding—and they were leaving in just a few days. With the good news—their home sold—they'd stay in South Carolina for a couple of weeks and look for a home there before returning home.

And guess what?

Yep! They found their perfect home! But it would be a contingency sale; that couple would need to find another home before they could sell. And that is exactly what happened.

So many moving pieces but everything seemed to be divinely orchestrated.

As part of our acceptance, our realtor told us, we'd need to provide proof of funds within five days. Apparently, now that we were in contract, our realtor had multiple parties wanting to purchase the home. We were told that each of these parties had been in the mix for quite some time—watching and waiting for continued price reductions.

Few homes in Coeur d'Alene and the surrounding areas were at this price point.

Maybe they lost out because of greed—it would cost nearly double to build the home compared to what the couple was asking for the home.

Or maybe it was simply, God! In fact, God had intervened and held His hand to protect the couple from moving to Florida and getting wiped out—more about this later. God had ever so patiently waited for us to figure out . . . we weren't building a home. He had a home waiting for us all along.

Unfortunately for those buyers sitting on the fence, consideration (money) would not be an issue for my husband and I; we would not be falling out of escrow.

Once again, I think we might have surprised our realtor with our response regarding proof of funds. We told him, we were already pre-qualified with a local banker in Coeur d'Alene; I gave him his name. And, yep, he knew the banker; they'd gone to high school together. This really was a small town.

A couple of days later, our banker sent the realtor a proof of funds letter and we were officially in contract.

Since we were in escrow, it was time to contact the builder and tell him our news. I am big on respecting others and their time. I knew Rosenberger had already cashed our $7,000 check to restart our project—preliminary drawings; so I could only assume that his architect had re-started our project.

But this time, instead of calling, I'd send him an email. Shelley replied, she was very gracious and congratulated us on our purchase. She also mentioned that she'd send us any refund due. One week later, we received a check.

Consideration

Now it was time to finance the home.

Again, thank you, Susie and Jurgen for selling our home in Santana Row so quickly and for top dollar—four months ago.

Thank you, Uncle Jimmy, for your inheritance.

Thank you, Gilead, for issuing stock dividends and alerting Marine County to their oversight; one of Uncle Jimmy's stocks had split during the three years Marine County was probating his estate.

Thank you, Marine County, for opening up a second probate and then, again, taking another year and a half for distribution of funds—two months ago.

Talk about timing! Obviously, we are very blessed.

Then it happened again . . . well, almost.

Shortly after our offer was accepted, our realtor listed our lot for sale. A week later, he called us back; he told us we must be very, very blessed. We were intrigued? He explained that he already had a couple that was interested in purchasing our lot.

Well, between the sale of our loft, the second inheritance, and now the money for the lot, we would be able to pay cash for the home without dipping into our investments.

But before they'd make an offer, they wanted to send their builder out to dig some test holes on the land before they committed. We agreed. Afterwards, this deal would fall through and we would take out a small mortgage on our home.

Although my husband seemed a bit eager to sell our land, I was not. I felt at great peace in "knowing," whatever was supposed to happen with our lot, would happen in God's perfect timing. One year later, we'd let the listing expire.

Meanwhile, my husband was excited! He, too, had fallen in love with Coeur d'Alene and now we were homeowners there—well, almost. We were only in escrow, so technically the home was still not ours. In addition, we made the decision that he would not give notice until after escrow closed. If we were applying for a mortgage, he'd need to show that he was still employed. Nevertheless, my husband couldn't contain his enthusiasm.

Inasmuch, back at work, one of his colleague's had overheard him talking about the home in Coeur d'Alene we were purchasing. The colleague was curious and stopped by. After seeing the pictures up on my husband's computer screen, he blurted out: "Hey, that's my house! You purchased my house!" He told my husband, he had been tracking the activity on the home for nearly two years!

Title and First Look

Back in Coeur d'Alene . . . a week later . . . the next day, our realtor picked my husband and I up from our hotel, and took us to the title company where we closed escrow.

Next, he took us to the Assessor's Office where we filed our homeowner's exemption paperwork. A homeowner's exemption is a program that reduces property taxes for individuals who own and occupy their home as their primary residence. This is done by reducing the net taxable value of the home and up to one acre of land by half (up to a certain maximum).

Thereafter, he dropped us off downtown where we met back up with Scott and Susan.

The following day, our realtor picked us up again; but this time Scott and Susan would join us. He was taking us to see our new home for the first time. We were beyond excited! From the panoramic views of Lake Coeur d'Alene to the scenic wooded home sites, The Ridge at Cougar Bay was a piece of heaven right next door.

As we made the drive up to The Ridge, to the top of the hill, just before we approached the driveway, we could see the "sold" sign prominently planted in the snow. This was a big deal up at The Ridge; we broke a record, purchasing this home for a record price of $1.5 million.

Then as we continued up the long winding narrow driveway, to the large private circular portion, we got our first glimpse of the home! We were blown away! It looked so different from the pictures and video— so much grander. Between the distant pictures on the internet and the video pictures with a yellow tint to them, there was no comparison.

More than likely, the flash didn't have enough power to reach far enough; even though the camera operator may have set the WB to the color of the flash, the light in the pictures was coming from the indoor lighting, which would cause a different color.

As we piled out of the Suburban, we were all speechless . . .

Then, at that moment—one of those moments in time that would change our lives forever—chills ran up and down my spine. God was speaking to me! This is what he had waiting for us. This was God's plan! He had been preparing me all along the way:

- When I was very young—seven- or eight-years-old—I had a vivid back-and-forth conversation with God Himself. Every week, me and my brothers went grocery shopping with my mother. And every week I would take a candy bar from the store and stuff it down my pants. (I'm repenting again as I am writing this.) But that last Saturday changed my life forever! At such a young age, I felt the conversation with God as real as speaking to my parents. I flushed that candy bar down the toilet and never took anything again. Ashamed, I never told anyone about it, until just now.

- Then, when I was nine-years-old, on my birthday, my parents gave me my first Bible: a red-letter King James Version. I am 60-something, and I still cherish that Bible today and base all my writings from it.

- Again, at ten-years-old, I remember looking at that stuffed raggedy Ann doll amongst the pillows on my bed, and bursting into tears uncontrollably. I wondered if that was all I was. As I pondered my own bleak destiny in utter despair, suddenly, I felt a calmness come over me. It was Him, again. God assured me that I was not that doll, I was His child. He also told me that I would one day deeply study the Bible and change lives.

- I was a self-proclaimed "information junky." In 1994, I started Step-by-Step Publishing, self-publishing several books before the Idiots Guide series and Dummies series.

- Thereafter, I pivoted to a career in law receiving my associate's degree in paralegal studies in 1996, my bachelor's degree in business administration in 1998, and my Juris Doctorate in law in 2002.

- In 2009, I started Aauvi House Publishing Group, self-publishing a memoir and business law books, and Fox Hunt Publishing Group for my husband's fiction works.

- In 2016, I surrendered to God . . . and have never once stopped reading and studying the Bible and extra-biblical works.

Academically I was prepared.

But now I needed my house in order to achieve a clear and calm state—before I could move on to other things . . . God blessed us with a sanctuary for me to reach such a mindset; a place we could age-in-place. I'd never need to move again! So I thought . . .

I was humble, passionate, trustworthy, and tenacious in everything I ever did; especially, when it came to God . . . and now, God would free me from any extracurricular obligations—raising kids, caregiving for my husband's parents (may all three rest in peace) and then for my own parents—which, would soon be fulfilled, too.

Then, it would be up to me: I'd need to make good on my promise that I made with God nearly eleven years ago.

As we approached the oversized glass front door, I couldn't believe that it had a life-sized metal tree fastened to it! We'd learn, that the couple had commissioned a local artist he knew, and it'd taken her a year to finish. I was in love with trees! I owned 31 fruit and nut trees, which were now staged at my parent's house! I fell in love with the forest trees after we crossed the Idaho border!

This truly was a personal touch from God!

It was beyond gorgeous; it's branches even extended to the glass side door windows—interior and exterior. In the center of the tree trunk, it had a realistic large tree knot. Later, we'd learn that the knot was replicated from the living room fireplace wood mantel knot—this couple had exquisite taste.

Then, more drama: looking right through the glass front door—through the foyer, through the living room—you could see the Lake City; Lake Coeur d'Alene, Lake Coeur d'Alene Resort, and downtown Coeur d'Alene. The view was spectacular; you didn't even need to go inside the house to see it all.

In fact, the entire property—1.13 acres—enjoyed this view. The thought that went into the building, design, and positioning of this home was both beautiful and dramatic in an eye-catching way. This house was unique. This house was special. This was a house from God!

As the door opened, our realtor introduced us to the couple. And bless their hearts, he had Parkinson disease, among other things, and she had multiple sclerosis. He used walking sticks and she used a walker. But you could not meet a more lovelier, livelier, sweeter couple. Her nickname for him was also very enduring, "Sugar."

But because of health reasons, they both wanted to move to a warmer climate, and so they were anxious for their home to sell—the last few winters had been unusually harsher than normal.

We'd also learn that initially they thought they'd move to Florida—but they thanked "the sweet Lord" their house did not sell early on. Had they moved to Florida, in the area they'd chosen, they would have been wiped out by a hurricane losing everything.

And then, our tour began . . . Sierra Pacific wood windows and doors throughout—85 windows, Acacia hardwood floors with inlays in the foyer, living room, and kitchen. Oversized four-car heated garage with Bendpak car lift. And incredible landscaping; the circular driveway even had a five foot circular centerpiece: a decorative hardscape compass in the middle of it reading: N, E, S, W.

It was all very overwhelming; at one point, my husband and I, excused ourselves to the outside deck, as we shed a few very happy tears. We were home! This was where we were supposed to be!

Thank you Almighty God!

Reflecting back, our family and friends thought we were crazy to purchase a home sight unseen. But we trusted in God, and He over delivered! We are truly blessed. Not to mention, had the unexpected second inheritance not come through, we would never have been able to afford this home without liquidating our investments.

We are blessed indeed!

New Beginnings and Lifelong Friendships

8

Back in California . . . a month after we closed escrow on our new home, I wanted to get in contact with the couple still living in our home. I had lots of questions, since we had never owned a home this large (6,087 square feet) nor lived in a four-season environment. Our realtor told us this was an unusual request . . . but I pushed . . . and he made it happen. He was playing both sides: seller's representative and buyer's representative, which also meant double the commission; so I didn't mind asking for him to go the extra mile.

At first, we communicated with the couple through email. But then, after going back and forth for a while, I guess it was obvious that my questions weren't going to stop. I tried to pace myself; but I was excited and I had this sense that my time for questions and answers might have a deadline. Finally, probably out of pure exhaustion, the couple offered me their phone number; telling me it might be easier to handle my questions over the phone.

Suddenly, I felt awkward at the thought of calling; I may have fallen in love with them, but they were still strangers after all. So I waited until my husband came home from work before making the call.

That evening, we called and spoke to the couple over the phone. Immediately we hit it off; we actually had a lot in common. Both of our husbands had careers in defense. And her and I were both retired and enjoyed being homemakers, among other things. My husband was into the stock market; and so was she. Her husband loved stain glasswork and DIY projects; and I loved gardening and interior design projects.

They were also very happy and encouraged that we had so much interest in their home. This was the second home that they had built in Coeur d'Alene, but this one was their baby. But for health reasons, they would have never sold this home.

Then I pulled out my list of questions, and Q&A began . . . finally, more than likely out of more exhaustion, they told us we needed to come up to the house and stay with them for a few days. That way we could all go through the house together and they could educate us on the home.

We jumped at the chance!

Our agent was quite puzzled by this.

My husband and I, for some reason, didn't think this was strange at all—we'd do the same. This couple had built this home from the ground up, taught their builder much about design at the time, and had lived in the house for more than nine years. They knew more about this house than the realtor could ever have known.

Still, our agent claimed, he'd never heard of this before and thought it was a bad idea.

Hmmm . . . why would he think it was a bad idea?

Back in Coeur d'Alene . . . a week later . . . we'd make good on the invitation. This time, we would not be staying in a hotel; instead, we'd stay—for the very first time—in our home along with the couple. We arrived by cab and the couple warmly greeted us.

They immediately invited us to sit down in the living room, which we obliged.

I sensed something was wrong. I also noticed she wasn't wearing her wedding ring.

They had questions:

First, they wanted to know, why we wanted housecleaners to come in before we moved in?

The house was immaculate.

She was concerned; she told the realtor, she would not allow any housecleaners to be scheduled without meeting them beforehand in person—they had lots of art in the house and had prior issues with cleaning people in the past.

I explained, that I did not think housecleaners were necessary; and I, too, would not want anyone in my home that I had not met before.

She seemed relieved.

I told her I would talk to the realtor and tell him to cancel any pending appointments.

Next, they told us that they had people showing up at the door; telling them that it was okay for them to come through the house and take measurements.

These were probably some of those buyers that missed out on the purchase of the home; wanting to copy some of the design.

Of course, they turned them away. But after doing so, they wondered if this was really something we authorized?

We again, told them, absolutely not and thanked them for not letting the people in. I then further assured the couple that we'd back them up one hundred percent on all decisions—we'd never agree to something without their knowledge.

Then they wanted to know how we discovered the house. They told us the realtor told them, he found us.

This didn't really surprise me; after all, he was in the sales business.

We explained, we'd become friendly with the neighbors, Dan and Joleen, and when we were frustrated with our build, we called Dan. During our conversation, Dan blurted out, "Why don't you just buy Bill and Jess's house?" We had no idea this house was on the market because we weren't looking for a house; we were building a home, or so we thought.

I further explained, we called the realtor right away, exchanged contact information, and he sent us the 3D house tour drone video. We were immediately sold and called the realtor the next day—we told him we wanted to make an offer on the house for full ask and asked him if he could also represent us.

The couple didn't seem to be surprised to hear the truth; they mentioned that although the realtor had their listing for more than two years—this last attempt to sell—they almost didn't re-list with him.

Other things were going on, too . . .

The realtor told us that his son does the yard work for the home; we learned this was not true. However, the agent's son did snowplow the driveway once, recently—but when he did, he broke one of the landscaping lights and then didn't tell anyone.

We'd help replace the light fixture during this stay with the couple.

Funds were still being held back in escrow. There was a minor portion of the home that still needed to be re-stained where the homeowner could not reach. The realtor had hired a person to do the job; however, that person was rude to Bill, which created great stress for him. The painter also wanted way too much money for such a small job.

I explained that I would handle everything and for the two of them not to worry about anything.

Now that we were all on the same page, we were shown to the room they had made up for us downstairs. Then, they gave us cart blanche and told us to enjoy the home as if we already lived there.

All in all, our visit was a wonderful experience. They showed us around town, around the house and yard, and introduced us to neighbors, special friends, as well as many others. We even purchased some of their furniture to be left behind.

Then, on our last day, I noticed, she was wearing her wedding ring—it was lovely! Bill was even comfortable enough to open the gun safe and show my husband some of his private collections.

Not only did we have tons in common, we really weren't that far apart in age either, and quickly became lifelong friends.

Unfortunately, Bill would pass away in March the following year. She'd move back to the west coast with her brother and his wife; and she'd tell me later, she was now close enough where her son also visited her monthly. She is a lovely, beautiful, kindhearted soul, whom I'm very blessed to call my friend. To this day, we keep in touch, send pictures back and forth, share a love for hummingbirds and hopefully someday she'll be able to come back and visit.

On our way home, in the airplane, I drafted an email to the realtor and blind copied the couple when I sent it. I was kind and let everyone save face. Going forward, I would handle anything that needed the realtor in the loop for.

Taking Care of Loose Ends

Back in California . . . I started looking to hire movers. During my search I found out three things: first, movers charge by the weight; second, movers will not take a car; and third, movers will not guarantee delivery dates. They'll give you a window, but according to most of the reviews that I read, the window is usually twice as long as they estimate.

This meant, in addition to hiring a moving company to transfer our belongings to Idaho, we'd also need to hire a second carrier to transport our second car—transporting the car could take up to a couple of months before we'd receive it.

So of course, I called the couple back. She had given me a date when their movers would be moving them. So I asked her if she had a moving company referral. Of course she did; her and her husband had moved many times before with a private company—since his job required it. She gave us the name of her movers and I called.

Interestingly, before I could get any information from them, they needed to know how I found them. After I told them who referred us to them, they were more than happy to help us. Not only would they commit to an exact delivery date, they'd also take the car along with all of our stuff in the same moving truck. This was fantastic news!

Thank you Jess! Thank you Jesus!

On another front, my husband was stressing about having to give notice and possibly having to leave his dream job. Ideally, he hoped he could continue working with the company remotely. He had only been back a little over a year and now we were moving.

Nonetheless, I told him, he needed to bite the bullet and do the right thing. He needed to give his employer as much notice as possible. It was mid-March and that would give his boss a couple of months' notice before we moved.

So the very next day, reluctantly, he gave notice to his employer. His manger took it well—but really liked his work. He had a brilliant mind and a large network following within the company. Inasmuch, she did go to bat for him—but as it played out, company policy didn't allow employees to work from home.

Instead, however, they worked out a deal where he could still work with his employer—but as a contractor, through the contracting services company his employer exclusively used. This meant no 1099s, no quarterly taxes, just a standard W-2 at the end of the year. It was perfect!

So he and the two companies decided on the following: a termination date for his employer, a start date with his new employer— the contracting service company—and an agreed upon wage that both companies agreed to.

Once again, my husband was generous with his time. Instead of asking for top dollar, which he could have gotten, he settled for a moderate wage, which, nonetheless, would still double his take home pay. In the state of California he was in a more than 50-percent tax bracket. As a resident of the state of Idaho, taxes were a lot different—

much, much lower. Not to mention the lower cost of living in the Northwest.

This would be his third windfall in less than two years: six months' severance after a layoff, second inheritance, and now this contracting job.

My husband's new contracting work, coupled with our move to Idaho, would also add years to his life. Commuting to and from work every day from Santana Row to Sunnyvale had turned my—otherwise easy going—husband into a five star road ragger! Everyone gets mad now and again while driving; but he'd get particularly aggressive or angry.

I knew this, because he'd call me every day on his way home from work and we'd talk until he finally arrived home an hour later.

I thought his driving temper would get better when we moved to Sunnyvale—he had barely a commute at all—but I'd be mistaken.

Thank you God! In Idaho, his commute is simply a short flight of stairs downstairs to his office.

Now I was a much more patient driver. When living in Santana Row, my commute to my parents was only four miles away and was a very relaxed drive. Then we sold our home in Santana Row and moved to Sunnyvale; now my commute was an hour drive to and from my parent's house each morning and then again, each night—even though, they only lived nine miles away.

So on top of my caregiving services from 9:00 a.m. to 5:00 p.m. four days a week; I was actually spending 40-plus-hours a week on my self-imposed extracurricular obligation to my parents.

Insofar as my behavior on the road, externally I remained a peaceful and calm driver. But internally, these added hours on the road only increased my ever growing to do list. I never had enough time to get things done. Consequently, I was becoming an internally stressed out driver, myself.

Then there was my parents to deal with in between my travels. My mother was becoming more and more angry that I was moving; she felt abandoned and she was taking it out on me. I was starting to feel more like I was disposable than a daughter.

And my father's health wasn't getting any better, which meant more work for mom. In return, all my father wanted to do was to make mom happy, which meant asking me to do more and more things: taking the garbage cans to and from the home, picking fresh oranges off the tree daily, filling the pond with water daily, making coffee (something I could never get right, seemingly), chopping and pre-packaging fresh vegetables, steaming vegetables, cooking breakfast burritos for my dad's daily breakfast, ordering roses for her ahead of time for Mother's Day (even though she wasn't his mother), etc.

This was on top of all the errands, medical meetings, shopping trips, and anything else my mom wanted to do.

Then there was my 31 fruit and nut trees—in portable pots—in her backyard that I needed to water every day; that summer was a hot one.

She still had no intention of moving; and later, I'd learn, secretly she wondered if she'd ever see me again—this made me sad.

I needed to do something, I felt like I was failing as a daughter . . .

Then, I had an "ah ha" moment.

I'd discuss it with my husband before I'd break the news to my mom. She'd had been wanting to visit her sister in Washington, but couldn't because of my dad's health problems—and her sister couldn't visit her because of her own health issues.

So I thought . . . maybe, if I told her: after the move we'd drive back to California—four weeks later, after we got settled in—to pick her, dad, and Molly (their dog) up and bring them to our new home. During their stay, her sister and my uncle could also come up for a visit in their motor home. My parent's would stay three weeks through the fourth of July holiday—to enjoy the fireworks celebration from our deck—at our home. Afterwards, we'd drive them back to California.

After clearing this with my husband, I gave my mom the good news. She suddenly was happy again; I'd gotten my mom back. She was excited; she had something to look forward to.

She immediately called her sister and both of them began trip-planning mode. My dad was excited, too.

Now both my parents would see our beautiful new home and fall in love with Coeur d'Alene. Then, just maybe, they'd agree to move—either move in with us or move into an independent assisted living community close by.

And just like that, another blessing, the phone rang. It was the couple we purchased our home from. She had an electric wheelchair that probably only needed batteries and wanted to know if we wanted it. She knew that my father was in a transport chair and could use it when they visited. What she didn't know was how soon my parents would be coming to visit. We thanked them and gratefully accepted their generous gift.

On to the next order of business . . . my trees! I had been going back and forth with the Idaho State Department of Agriculture with respect to transporting my trees cross country—but I was getting nowhere.

This problem would solve itself. It became a moot point, when our moving company informed us they would not be able to transport the trees. However, they would transport the oversized pots and wheels thereon as long as I had also gotten rid of all the soil. Well that kind of summed it up: I'd need to find a new home for my trees.

I'd need to start over in Coeur d'Alene.

Mom came to my rescue—she had an arborist that had been working with her trees and koi fishponds for more than 30-years. She made the call and he agreed to send a team down to gut the pots and take the trees. Thereafter, his guys would wheel the heavy pots back to the end of the backyard—where they'd sit until the movers picked them up. In the meantime, there were three trees that my mother wanted to keep: the apricot tree, the plum tree, and the peach tree—each were about twelve to fifteen feet tall.

Finally, we'd give notice 30-days before our move, which was also ten weeks prior to our lease expiring. But, since our apartment complex and location was in such high demand, they re-rented our unit and we had no extra out of pocket expenses for breaking our lease.

On our last two nights in California, we'd stay with my parents.

Loading Up

It was move day . . . and the tractor-trailer truck was huge! But it was also the prettiest tractor-trailer I've ever seen; it looked brand new. So that also meant they'd need to rent a local bobtail moving truck, to transport everything that was in our storage unit to the main tractor-trailer truck—it was parked in a large transport yard—that was day one.

Day two, they drove that oversized tractor-trailer truck to our apartment complex and loaded everything therein into the truck as well. How they maneuvered that truck in and out of the streets of downtown Sunnyvale, I'll never know. But they did so, flawlessly.

Then, still that same day, they drove the bobtail truck to my parent's house and picked up all twenty-eight pots—each carefully wrapped in cargo blankets. Finally, on day three, we drove our Corvette to the transport yard where our moving truck was parked and a tow truck loaded it. Everything we owned was in that truck!

After everything was loaded, for a moment it felt eerily final . . . Then I snapped out of it! I trusted in Jesus, so there was no reason to feel nervous. Instead, I shutdown those pesky demons of Satan that were trying to get into my head. I was leaving California! Satan would no longer have a hold on me. I had God the Holy Spirit in my heart that Christ left me when he ascended to heaven after his first coming! Inasmuch, I no longer live in fear—I trust our Lord Jesus Christ.

Our final stop, an appointment at the Goodyear Tire dealership. We had just gotten our four-wheel drive Lexus GX 470 out of the shop for any maintenance it may have needed before our long road trip to Idaho. And now it was time for new tires; we were putting "all-weather tires" on our car. All-weather tires are much better than all-season tires in the winter, while performing significantly better in the summer when compared to winter tires. We wanted to be prepared for the four-season environment we were moving to.

The next morning, we'd start our road trip to Coeur d'Alene . . .

Home Sweet Home

Back to Coeur d'Alene . . . our road trip to our new home was uneventful. On our first leg, we drove from California to Bend, Oregon and stayed overnight there; we took our time and stopped at most rest stops—ten hours. On our last leg, we'd drive straight through to Coeur d'Alene, again stopping at most rest stops, which would take another eight hours. We'd arrive on Mother's Day!

Along the way, I couldn't help it—I was having great anxiety about the home being left alone; almost a panic attack. The couple was scheduled to be out of the house a few days before we arrived. And then there was the fact that the house had been on the market for a couple of years. And what happened to those buyers who were hoping we'd fall out of escrow? And what about the people, who showed up at the door, wanting to take measurements inside the house after we'd purchased it? And would all the furniture we'd purchased from the couple still be there? After they left, would someone come back into the house, thinking it was left behind because they didn't want it?

I needed to stop this train of thought! It was making me crazy!

Then my phone rang . . . it was her . . . it was the couple we purchased the house from. As it turned out, they had bitten off more than they could chew and needed a few extra days in the home; they hadn't left yet! Literally, when we finally drove up to our new home, they and their movers had just pulled away from the home a couple of hours prior. Their timing couldn't have been more perfect!

Strategically, we had purchased one of the downstairs bedroom sets, so we had a place to sleep. Our movers would not be arriving until two days later. We were also exhausted so we stayed in and took in the house that first night.

The next day, we'd spend the day knocking out my to do list: unload the car, laundry, grocery shopping, banking—we wanted cash on hand so we'd have tip money for our movers the next day. Then there was the 810 square foot man cave, the bonus room above the garage, that needed to be filled—so we went to Priano's Billiards and Backyards and ordered an eight foot pool table with custom (indigo) felt, poker table and chairs, and five-piece bar set and barstools.

At Priano's, the owner, liked our dog—she's a small shih poo, part Shih Tzu, part poodle—her name is GiGi. Then out of nowhere, he asked us if we had a veterinarian.

At the time, we thought this was odd—we had arrived just 24-hours ago. But in my walk with God, I've learned to pay attention! So I told him, we didn't have a vet yet, we'd just moved to Coeur d'Alene. So he voluntarily told us of an animal hospital that he highly recommended. I wrote it down and we thanked him.

But, what I didn't know was how soon I'd need this information.

We had a 3:00 p.m. deadline so we needed to get home. I had pre-scheduled the locksmith to come over and change all the outside locks around the home—five doors. Again, we'd stay in that evening; I didn't want to leave our dog home alone . . . so I thought.

Then, around 4:30 p.m. that afternoon, I noticed GiGi seemed very lethargic and we were concerned. She wouldn't eat. She wouldn't drink water. She didn't even want a treat. So I called the vet Priano's recommended and we took her in. She was diagnosed with extreme dehydration and they wanted to keep her overnight to pump fluids in her. We agreed.

Movers Arrived

Early the next morning, the movers arrived—right on schedule.

First, the car was unloaded; they hired a tow truck company to come over and take it off the truck.

Next, they moved everything out of the third bay in the garage to the curb near the truck—this was leftover stuff from the couple that didn't fit in their truck. It was a blessing for all that we were using the same moving company. The movers would take the couple's things to them after our drop off.

Then they unloaded all 212 boxes—yes, I had an inventory sheet—stacking them in the empty third bay. All the furniture was moved into the house. Beds and exercise equipment were re-assembled and they were done.

The movers may have left—but we weren't done yet; we were still very worried about GiGi and missed her. She went everywhere with me: to my parent's, errands, shopping, dining, to the bar, and so forth. She even had her very own stroller.

So my husband and I rushed over to the vet and picked up our little girl. It actually turned out to be a blessing that she was there and not at the house when the movers were in and out. Looking back, I can't help but think that God had a hand in her circumstances . . .

And the Remodel Begins

Two days later, Pat, our friend—who just so happens to be a contractor—arrived from California. Since Coeur d'Alene was experiencing a shortage of day laborers, we thought we'd bring in our own people. Pat would be with us for two weeks. The next day, Ditra would also arrive to help—Pat's assistant and also our friend. She'd stay for one week. Pat and Ditra would be comforting for our GiGi, too; she knew them both well.

I needed to get my house in order so that I could move on to bigger and better things—God was being very patient with me. This was a very different home from the home I was designing and shopping for.

It would need to be functional—two offices, bed and breakfast wing for guests, gym or exercise area(s), lower level kitchenette and space for my parents (in-law suite), accommodations for our indoor dog (kennel, eating, and washable potty pad areas), indoor garden area in the last bay of the garage for a solarium: a room fitted with extensive areas of glass to admit sunlight in which plants are grown that need protection from cold weather, etc. This garage was perfect for a solarium! It had seven oversized windows, a back door with upper glass window, six windows in each of the three garage doors, and a Hot Dawg temperature controlled heater!

It would also need to be designed for entertaining—three bars (one on each level), a kitchenette in the man cave, indoor-outdoor hangout spaces, sleeping rooms and areas—as designed, the home can sleep 25-people comfortably—and so on.

Finally, I'd need to incorporate my contemporary design style into the home, while still staying true to the traditional craftsman-style of the home.

This is also why we purchased some of the furniture and items from the couple we bought the home from—during our stay with them. For example, we purchased the oversized hall tree and built-in bench—five feet wide by eighteen inches deep by ten feet tall—in the foyer that was as tall as the glass front door; it had been pulled out of a New York brownstone in the late 1800s—the movers wanted $6,000 to move it; the consignment store appraised it at $12,000 in which he'd keep half.

Other items we purchased from the couple, included: two living room sofas—including coffee table, side table, and long narrow bench, main floor and lower level barstools, oversized mudroom bench and decorative scenic hooks (bear, elk, deer, and ducks) for hanging hats and coats, lower level bedroom set—bed, headboard, side table, dresser, and armoire, shower curtains—they were brand new and very fitting; the couple had hired an interior designer when they built the house.

We also purchased the snow blower and Universal gym that was in the garage.

And so the remodel began . . . first, we needed to get the man cave ready before the Priano's delivery. Pat gutted the man cave bathroom, which had been used as a work area: out with the sink, countertops, and toilet—he'd need to replace the floor as well.

Next, he removed the door, door trim, and all the baseboards (inside and outside) from the wall that we would be placing the two-piece bar up against. Then, he closed up the wall. Ditra then primed and painted the wall. He then cut a new point of entry around the corner at the man cave entrance, and re-installed the door and door trim there. He'd also install new temporary flooring in the bathroom before replacing all the baseboards inside and outside of the space. Finally, he re-installed the toilet and installed a new vanity and mirror above the sink.

Now the man cave was ready for the Priano's delivery as well as had space for a full size refrigerator-freezer on the same wall. Later—post-Pat—we'd rip out the temporary laminate flooring, install two waterlines for the refrigerator-freezer and future ice machine, before laying tile down in the bathroom.

Next, Pat would replace all the florescent lighting in the man cave and bathroom therein with cam lighting and a pool table light fixture above the pool table. The cam lighting, however, would too, turn out to be a temporary solution. After my husband spent a day in his new man cave, he informed me there was not enough lighting up there.

So I put it on the schedule—post-Pat—to hire electricians to remove the existing cam lights; then, reposition and add more of them throughout the room. The pool table light fixture installed by Pat would also need to be moved. My husband also decided there was not enough room around the pool table so I had the Priano's guys come back out and re-position the pool table. I'd also end up replacing the cam light in the bathroom with a light fixture.

In the meantime, all the walls and carpet in the home were the color beige—6,087 square feet. I needed to add life to the home! So Ditra and I got started on painting rooms and accent walls throughout the home: man cave accent back wall—Modern Masters metallic statutory bronze, primary bedroom walls—dress blues, primary bathroom twenty-two foot high accent walls halfway up—dress blues, my office—teal, living room wall facing the lake view and dining room accent wall—Modern Masters metallic antique bronze, main floor half bathroom accent wall—red, first guest bedroom accent wall—Modern Masters metallic warm silver, second guest bedroom partial accent walls and ceiling—Modern Masters metallic gold, and third bedroom bathroom accent walls—navy blue.

In addition, Ditra repainted all the black iron tables and chairs out on the downstairs patio. I'd later install blue-and-silver designer carpet in the she cave—lower level oversized unfinished storage room—and finish the space.

Now that I had added color to the home, next were mirrors to add drama and capture the beauty outside, inside. Pat moved the living room light switch panel, AC controls panel, and wiring—off the living room wall that faced the lake view—around the corner to the foyer wall; he then mounted my three oversized Timber Leaner Mirrors—peach 30-inches wide by 3-1/4-inches deep by 78-inches high—five inches apart and two feet above the floor. Now everywhere you turned in the living room you could see the gorgeous lake view and downtown Coeur d'Alene.

Next, Pat changed out the florescent lighting in the she cave and master walk-in closet with chandeliers; he replaced the ceiling lights in the three downstairs bedrooms with combination ceiling fans and lights, and added a ceiling fan in the primary bedroom upstairs.

He inspected our roof and attic spaces and made a few minor repairs—in addition to several war tours, Pat had also been a roofer for 30-years.

He also re-built the downstairs barstools, dining room table, and platform bed; this was something the movers did not get right—the bed fell to the floor our first night.

He also did a new light installation above the art wall cutout in the lower level. Then hung all of our art pieces on both the lower level and main floor. He even helped my husband set up his new gas barbeque on our deck.

Believe it or not, 5:00 p.m. would be our cutoff time; we'd head downtown for dinner, drinks, and pool. Meeting Pat and Ditra after our move to Sunnyvale was truly a blessing. Quickly, Pat became close to my husband; he even taught him his pool game back in California. He would become a lifelong friend.

But I wasn't done yet. Next, the dining room accent wall; I'd later install five more mirrors thereon—three forming an arch and two rectangle mirrors ten inches apart on either side of the arch—all above the butlers buffet cabinet. Now instead of that wall being a dead end dining room wall, it actually brought the forest outside into the interior of the home. It was official; our home in the spring/summer time felt more like we lived in a fishbowl. In the fall/winter, it felt like we lived inside a snow globe. It all seemed very majestic; I could see our home coming together.

The only real issue the house fell short on was the primary walk-in closet; I guess California women have much more stuff. I'd reconfigure the primary walk-in closet, converted the two linen closets in the primary bathroom to more closet space, and grabbed the walk-in closet downstairs in the third bedroom—my husband was using as his office—for my coats and hats to make it work and create functionality.

Last, I'd bring the greenery into and throughout the home.

Family, Friends, and God

Back to California . . . true to my word, I needed to stop working on our house and make the drive to pick up my parents and their dog, Molly. Of course, GiGi went with us. She loves Molly!

Back to Idaho . . . Again, our road trip to and from was uneventful. My parent's fell in love with our home; how could they not? We dined, shopped, and showed them the town; and surprisingly, my mother even put down a deposit at one of the independent assisted living sites we looked at.

As planned, my mom's sister and my uncle also came up for a visit during my parents stay. Unfortunately, this would be the last time I'd ever see my aunt. After 17-years, her illness took her life three weeks later. It was truly a blessing to be able to visit with her before she passed; thank you, Jesus.

Shortly after they left, Scott and Susan came up for the fourth of July holiday. Fireworks were so much more spectacular from our deck as compared to what we experienced the previous year—on the green in front of the Coeur d'Alene Resort—too much smoke, too many people, and too much traffic!

Back to California . . . three weeks may have been a bit too much for all of us but we got my parents and Molly back home safely.

Back to Idaho . . . my husband was really a good sport! He was also a very good driver. We were also happy knowing that we could take GiGi on long road trips without having to hospitalize her. She never had another episode. The only thing we could think of, was maybe the stress of the move? But maybe . . . simply . . . God thought she needed a break? Being there with the movers would have only added more stress to her already stressed out self.

Back at home, life continued on . . . I took my notes from our stay with the couple we bought the home from and dissected the house.

For the next few months, our driveway would be busy with the comings and goings of electricians, plumbers, HVAC servicemen, handymen, security personnel, home theater people, elevator guys, appliance repairmen; gutters cleaned, windows cleaned, driveway power washed; additional window covering installations; screen doors serviced, landscapers—mow and blow; even cutting down a tree that was blocking one of the guest room's view—you name it; everyone was in and out of the house. Hence, the real reason I did not feel it was necessary to deep clean our home until it was done.

Nonetheless, I needed to pause, GiGi was low maintenance but now she seemed unhappy and bored; I was too busy and not paying enough attention to her. Then she started having accidents in the house. She was trying to get my attention.

I thought about it and realized, what she really needed was a friend. So we got her a puppy, Kaiya—an Alaskan Klee Kai (miniature husky). The puppy solution was perfect! She will definitely add years to her life. We've never seen her more playful and happy.

And now we've learned, we will always have two dogs.

At the same time, I kept my interior design and party planner hats on too. As to the former, I was still unpacking, changing and moving things around, shopping (I had a house to fill), and preparing our home for a lifetime of celebrations. As for the latter, I outdid myself:

- I threw my husband his first football party in his man cave.

- I hosted Thanksgiving for family and friends. Scott and Susan even made the move to Coeur d'Alene after all.

- In the middle of December, I hosted—what would become an annual event—our holiday party.

- The following year, I'd host a combined birthday party for my husband and one of his new friends he'd met downtown— whose birthday was the same weekend.

- I'd even host our second fourth of July party inviting more friends and neighbors.

- In between, we had and continue to have many out of town guests visiting off and on.

My husband even named his man cave, Tavern at The Ridge. Our home had become truly a hot spot. We were truly blessed and grateful for everything and everyone in our lives, but mostly to our heavenly Father, our Lord Jesus Christ.

And then COVID hit us hard . . .

God's Calling

Two years later, I understood clearly God's calling. God had been preparing me throughout my life, even before 2016, when I threw my arms up and "surrendered" myself to His will:

> "Father, if you are willing, remove this cup from me: nevertheless not my will, but your will be done" (Luke 22:42).

What did Jesus mean when He said to the Father, not my will but your will, be done? It is called the prayer of consecration. It means, we should prioritize what God wants in our lives and be open as He guides us on a journey, we may not have otherwise pictured ourselves on. In other words, God has a purpose for each of our lives, even when we don't understand. But His plan is always better than any plan that we could ever form in our own hearts.

Since 2016, I've continued to be willing and obedient—following God's plan for my life—praying the prayer of consecration daily. As a result, God has blessed my husband and I with so much more than we could have ever imagined: a blessed extended family, a peaceful state to live in, a beautiful home, and health; and now it was just me, my husband, and our two dogs—no more obstacles in my life.

My parents decided to stay in their home in California a little while longer before moving to Florida where my father could remain in his own (new) home there without the costs. I had passed my caregiving torch over to my three brothers, and they also, were willing and obedient (more about this later).

I finally had time to myself. And at that moment, I instantly knew exactly what God had called me to do!

Now, I had time to fulfill my part of the covenant, I had made with Him back in 2007, when death knocked at my door. I promised: I'll do anything you ask, just please let me live to finish raising my teen boys. He kept His Word and now it was my time to fulfill my part, my promise. At that moment, I instinctively knew, I would be entering into the next phase of the rest of my life—walking with God.

I had discovered God's plan for my life—my true purpose in life—to follow God and do his works. My mission: an in-depth study of God and the Bible and this is what The Ridge Publishing Group is all about: focusing on God and the Bible while creating and designing new and fresh ways for learning, teaching and understanding in books, textbooks, documentaries in print, board games and card decks. My mission is to prepare and motivate people to live for eternity.

For more information about The Ridge Publishing Group you can visit the website at https://www.RidgePublishingGroup.com.

Launching The Ridge Publishing Group—evangelizing and spreading the word of our Lord Jesus Christ in novel ways—and its imprints is one of the five single moments in time that would change my life forever.

In our new home, my husband never missed a beat. Not only did he continue contracting exclusively with his dream job—the work, for the most part, just kept pouring in. When he had lulls, he'd be right back at re-working his book series, Ethan Fox Books.

We live life with the understanding that we have more than enough; the more we give of ourselves, the more we receive—the more we willingly and obediently follow God's plan (not our own) the more blessed we become.

> "Give, and it will be given to you. Good measure, pressed down, shaken together, running over, will be put into your lap. For with the measure you use it will be measured back to you" (Luke 6:38).

After COVID, I often found myself pondering, why did God want us in such a big house or on such a large piece of property? I guess, one day, we'll discover the answer . . . Likewise, because of the state of the world, it caused lulls in my husband's work, so we also decided to re-list our lot for sale. We thought, whether it sells or not . . . it's up to God. It sold! I also finally convinced my husband that he did not need to work for anyone else anymore, he needed to solely use his God-given talent, writing fantasy fiction—The Ridge Publishing Group's, Ethan Fox Books imprint. I have full faith and trust in our Lord Jesus Christ in everything that happens.

Along my journey, while writing books for The Ridge Publishing Group imprint: Guardians of Biblical Truth, and the New Narrated Study Bible (NNSB); I also found my church! Funny, how we always seem to be so quick to judge; a bad habit of mine that Jesus keeps bringing to my attention.

Early on, we often drove by this church—it was located off a main highway—but it didn't have much curb appeal. At first, I wasn't interested in it at all; ignorantly, because the name of the church is Candlelight Christian Fellowship, I assumed it offered nighttime services only. I hated the idea of "church shopping" it just didn't seem right. So I contacted our neighbor, Joleen, and asked for her recommendations. One of which, was Candlelight; she had friends that attend it. There it was! It was my validation! Not only did Candlelight have traditional Sunday morning services, it was a Christian church, it preached solely from the Bible.

After a couple of months attending Candlelight, since I hadn't been in church for years, I initially had mixed feelings about the church. I loved the Christian rock band, I loved the pastor, I loved the people, it had plenty of security—but I found myself questioning the format. Pastor Paul seemed to only preach during the last half of the service.

Then it happened again . . . without thinking . . . one day out on the town, I found myself blurting out to a girlfriend: "At the rate our pastor preaches, it'll take him ten years to get through the Bible." (Obviously, I was still a baby Christian.) This statement also immediately caused me to question the church—apparently; I had let Satan and his demons into my head. Later that night, I realized it wasn't Candlelight that was the issue. It was my behavior, judging again! I needed to stop and repent! I felt horrible and remorseful . . . so the next time I saw my girlfriend, I called myself out and apologized.

As a result, I fell in love with my church all over again. Candlelight, Pastor Paul, and the entire church community are all amazing people. Coincidentally, Pastor Paul and my husband also had something in common. They both were from the Sacramento area; during our initial meet and greet, they talked about the high schools they attended and the likes. My husband was sold from that day on! He looked forward to attending church on Sundays with me.

A couple of months later, I'd do another obedient act showing God and the world my commitment to Jesus Christ. Pastor Paul water baptized me in front of the whole congregation—full immersion.

Susan, Scott, and Daniel (another friend) attended my baptism and afterwards, we celebrated at breakfast. This was truly a very special day for me. For this, I am forever grateful to the Candlelight Church family.

Mom, Listening to God

As it turned out . . . my parents did move; they sold their house in California and purchased a new home in Florida, near my brothers. Initially, I'd find out about their plans by accident—my mom sent a text to me that was meant for one of my brother's in Florida. At first I was crushed! I felt betrayed . . . I felt like everyone knew about their plans except me. I was angry!

Then, my husband and I rationally discussed it. Jesus was talking to me, too. He was telling me that their move was not about me. He was telling me that they'd have more help there and that it was my three brothers' turn to support them for now. I obediently called my mom, and we got back on track. Having things out in the open, made my father very happy as well.

From that point on, she continues to lean on me, which I love! For instance, when she was having issues with the California realtor—her Florida realtor found on the internet—to help them sell their home. She hadn't signed anything and now she wanted to have our friends, Susie and Jurgen, sell their home in California just like they'd done for us the year before. I was thrilled! Susie and Jurgen would take care of everything for them—they'd be in good hands.

Time was ticking . . . dad's strength was failing and my mom hurt her back pulling up dad; the doctors suggested rehab for six weeks. My parents initially struggled with this decision—but it, too, would turn out to be a blessing. This gave my mom time to heal, search for a new home in Florida, and get her home ready for sale.

In her despair, I told my mom: "God has a plan and always has. When you keep running into obstacles and things continue to go wrong, you are not following His plan. On the other hand, if things are going well, you're probably on the right path following God's plan."

After rehab, dad did get some of his strength back; he'd be able to travel to Florida from California. Miraculously, they also found a newly built home that wasn't even on the market yet—just a couple of miles from one of my brother's. In fact, the builder was still living in the home. He needed to stay in it for two-years to avoid any tax consequences. It would be ready in a couple of months.

Then, Susie and Jurgen wanted my parents out of the house for open houses. This was causing tremendous stress for my mom—dad was no longer portable without a lot of help—so she talked to me. I told her, if it is causing you stress, don't do it. Just tell Susie and Jurgen, during open houses you'll stay in dad's room with Molly. And that's exactly what happened.

Then my parents got the bonus plan; my husband and I with our two dogs in tow would make one more road trip to California—we had a wedding to attend. They'd also get to see Kaiya for the first time. She also had some things she wanted us to have before she moved.

During our stay, she was stressing that they had already had several open houses but no offers; the homes in California had taken a downturn. In addition, she didn't have the funds to go into contract on the new home until her California home sold. And then there was the rent-back issue: She didn't want to have to pay rent to stay in the home after it sold—again, the Florida home would not be available until November tenth. She had a lot of moving parts going on.

I looked at her and told her, "you only need one buyer, it'll sell." I knew the home had curb appeal, the backyard was large, and it was located in a sought after area.

But my mom's stress continued to increase. She was also worried about the availability of last minute first class airline tickets—this was the only way she could transport dad. If her house didn't sell, she'd need to stay put, which also meant the possibility of losing the Florida home. She'd also need three tickets: one for my brother who would fly back and forth to help assist dad, then two more for her, dad, and Molly. I told her, she wouldn't have any problem.

Sure enough, a couple of days after we returned home, my mom called; they sold their house. In fact, their buyer even agreed to let them stay in the home "rent free" until they left for their new home in Florida. That sounded familiar; hadn't my husband and I done the same thing with the couple we purchased our house from?

Shortly after they closed escrow on their California home, they were in contract with the new home in Florida. This also meant, the builder could now commit to a move-out date so my parents could make their airline reservations. And, yep! She got the last three first class tickets on that plane.

God wanted her and dad in Florida with my brothers. God wanted my brothers to have a turn at caregiving for our parents. God wanted my time freed up so that I could do His works: evangelizing and writing books under the Guardians of Biblical Truth and the New Narrated Study Bible (NNSB) modern formats, and so much more.

In His Hands: A Life's Journey Reflecting God's Purpose

11

As I find a quiet moment to reflect upon the canvas of my life, I'm awestruck by the intricate design that God has painted through each of my experiences. "Total Surrender My Story" is more than just an autobiography—it's the embodiment of my faith, the realization that by surrendering wholly to God's will, I've discovered the path He intended for me all along.

It's easy to forget, especially in our fast-paced world, that God has a plan for each of us. The word "surrender" often conjures images of defeat or relinquishment. But in the context of my relationship with God, it's been about a beautiful submission—a yielding to a divine purpose greater than my own understanding.

Each chapter of this autobiography—Part One—represents a milestone in my spiritual journey. There were moments of doubt, where God's plan seemed elusive, and times of joy, where His presence felt palpably close. But in every chapter, in every experience, His hand was guiding, molding, and shaping me.

I've been blessed with myriad experiences—some challenging, other enriching but all divinely orchestrated. At times, I found myself questioning His ways, especially during moments of adversity. But looking back, I see the wisdom in every trial and the blessings in every storm. Every challenge was an invitation to draw closer to Him, and every victory was a testament to His endless grace.

The people God placed in my path, the lessons I was taught, the setbacks I encountered, and the triumphs I celebrated were all part of His grand design. Through each interaction, every tear shed, and every smile shared, God was teaching me something profound about my purpose and His love for me.

Now, with a heart brimming with gratitude, I acknowledge that every step, every stumble, every leap of faith was underpinned by His unwavering love. It's a humbling realization to recognize that even in moments of solitude, I was never truly alone. His presence was my constant, His word my guiding light.

Five Moments in Time that Changed My Life

In the grand tapestry of our lives, there are often defining threads that stand out, shimmering with divine significance. These threads aren't mere coincidences but divinely orchestrated moments where God gently steers our ship towards the purpose He has for us. As I look back, there are five such moments, each saturated with His presence, each reshaping my destiny in ways I could never have imagined.

1. **Married Eric in 2004**. Standing beside Eric on that sacred day in 2004, I wasn't just entering a covenant with him, but also with God. Our union wasn't merely the joining of two souls, but a divine partnership under the watchful eyes of our Creator. Every challenge, every joy, every shared dream was a testament to God's design for marriage: two become one. In Eric, I found not just a husband, but a partner in faith, a fellow traveler on this spiritual journey.

2. **Defeated Death in 2007**. 2007 brought with it a tempest that shook me to my core. Death didn't just knock; it loomed, casting shadows of doubt and fear. But in that bleak moment, I unearthed the profound secrets of prayer. It was no longer just a ritual but became a heartfelt conversation with God, a lifeline that connected me to His infinite grace. Through earnest supplication and unwavering faith, I felt God's hand pulling me from the abyss, reminding me that even in the darkest hour, He is the guiding light.

3. **Surrendered to God's Will in 2016**. By 2016, the lessons of life had taught me the beauty of surrender. I realized that true freedom wasn't about controlling my destiny but about yielding to God's will. In laying down my plans, my fears, and my desires at His feet, I discovered a purpose larger than myself. This surrender was not one of defeat, but of profound trust, an acknowledgment that God's plans for me were far grander than any I could envision.

4. **Moved from California to Northern Idaho in 2018**. Leaving the familiarity of California was not just a geographic shift but a spiritual journey. Northern Idaho, with its serene landscapes

and clear skies, seemed like a place handpicked by God. It was here, amidst the tranquility, that I felt God's voice more clearly, guiding me, molding me, and preparing me for the next chapter. The move wasn't just about a change in address; it was about planting roots in a place where God wanted me to bloom.

5. **Launched The Ridge Publishing Group in 2021.** The Ridge Publishing Group, and especially the imprint Guardians of Biblical Truth, wasn't just a business venture; it was a mission. The New Narrated Study Bible (NNSB) became a beacon, bringing the timeless message of our Lord Jesus Christ to people in fresh, engaging ways. Every word published, every story told, was a testament to God's word and a tool to evangelize His immense love. Through this endeavor, I felt God's calling, urging me to spread His message far and wide.

The five moments, while distinct in their experiences, share a common thread—the undeniable hand of God guiding, shaping, and blessing my journey. Looking back, I see not just the milestones of my life but the footprints of our Lord, reminding me that in every high and every low, He has been by my side. Each moment has been a stepping stone, leading me closer to understanding His purpose for me and serving as a testament to His unwavering love and grace.

As we transition into the next chapters—Part Two—which shares the wisdom and spiritual insights I've gleaned through my journey, my prayer is that my story serves as a testament to God's infinite love and purpose. May it inspire you to seek Him in every moment, to surrender wholly to His will, and to trust in His divine plan for your life.

Part Two

Total Surrender: Your Blueprint for a Meaningful Life

Your Life's Blueprint in Seven Steps

TOTAL SURRENDER

Your Life's True Calling Unraveling the Divine Blueprint

12

Picture this: a celestial tapestry, each thread woven with purpose and intention. That's God's grand design for us. We're not mere happenstances of the universe; we're meticulously planned, each of us bearing a distinct purpose. By divine intent, not human accident, you are here. A unique path waits your footsteps, a path leading to the most significant discovery of all: your true purpose in life. Intriguing, isn't it?

"For my thoughts are not your thoughts; neither are your ways my ways, declares the Lord" (Isaiah 55:8).

Isaiah 55:8 offers profound wisdom. It's a humbling revelation, one that often surprises many, especially if you've been amidst religious teachings. It's a common misconception, assuming that God's mindset mirrors ours. Yet, the deeper you delve into God's word, the clearer it becomes that His ways are beyond human comprehension.

Imagine walking a path with several forks, each choice representing our will and decisions. "I want this," "I choose that." Yet, with every determined step we take, there's a soft whisper reminding us of a different path, one not chosen by our compass but by a divine guide. More often than not, God's chosen direction for us is starkly different from our meticulously laid plans. This journey with Him is peppered with unexpected twists and thrilling revelations, all emphasizing the same truth: "my thoughts are not your thoughts; neither are your ways my ways."

So, how do you discern God's path in a world filled with endless choices? How do you know if that job, that place, or that relationship aligns with His divine purpose? The key lies in forging a deep connection with Him, seeking answers in the eternal wisdom of the Bible. As Isaiah 55:9 elucidates:

"For as the heavens are higher than the earth, so are my ways higher than your ways and my thoughts than your thoughts" (Isaiah 55:9).

Venturing into the labyrinth of life, guided by God's divine hand, is an adventure like no other. It's an exploration filled with discovery, surprises, and profound understanding. So, as you embark on this spiritual voyage to unearth your true calling, remember, it's not just about finding your purpose; it's about aligning with God's celestial plan for you. Ready to dive deep?

The Journey Isn't Always Linear

Like a river that winds, twists, and turns, sometimes we encounter rapids, and at other times, still waters. But therein lies the beauty of God's guidance. While we might perceive challenges as setbacks, in God's grand scheme, they are necessary detours, forging us into the individuals we're meant to be.

Have you ever felt a strong calling towards something, only to face obstacles at every turn? It's a test of faith, resilience, and surrender. These roadblocks are not necessarily signs of defeat, but rather checkpoints, asking us to pause, reflect, and reevaluate. Are we aligning our desires with God's intentions, or are we allowing our egos to take the wheel?

In our quest to decipher God's calling, patience is paramount. Unlike our fast-paced world that demands instant results, understanding God's purpose requires time, prayer, and a heart that listens more than it speaks. It's akin to piecing together a divine puzzle, where each piece, no matter how seemingly insignificant, has its perfect place.

Furthermore, the community around us plays a pivotal role. Surrounding ourselves with like-minded individuals, those who uplift our spirits and constantly guide us back to scripture, can be the beacon we often need. The wisdom of collective experiences, shared stories, and mutual faith creates a formidable force that not only strengthens our resolve but also fortifies our connection with God.

Concluding, let's embrace this journey of self-discovery and divine alignment wholeheartedly. As we continue to seek God's will and let His word illuminate our path, we'll find that the true secret to understanding our calling isn't just in the destination, but in every step, every choice, and every leap of faith we take along the way. So, with hearts open and faith unwavering, let's journey on, eager to experience all the surprises and blessings God has in store for us.

The Journey Brings Revelation

Every step forward in this divine journey brings with it a revelation. Some subtle, whispers of guidance; others, profound moments of clarity. Yet, the foundation of these revelations remains constant: trust in God's timing and plan.

Imagine life as a beautifully scripted play. Each act, scene, and dialogue is purposeful, leading to a transformative climax. But unlike a scripted play, where actors know their lines and endings, our lives thrive on faith. We might not know the next scene or how our story unfolds, but with God as the playwright, we're assured of a narrative filled with purpose, love, and growth.

In moments of doubt, when the path is obscured by fog and uncertainty, diving into the scriptures provides solace. Psalms, with its poetic verses, often resonates with our soul's yearnings, reminding us of God's enduring love and promise. Paul's letters in the New Testament reiterate the virtues of perseverance, the grace in waiting, and the strength derived from unwavering faith.

Connecting with nature, too, can serve as a spiritual reminder. The rhythmic patterns of the universe, from the rising and setting of the sun to the ebb and flow of tides, remind us of God's magnificent order in everything. Just as seasons change in a cyclical dance of transformation, our lives, too, undergo seasons—some of harvest and others of sowing, some of blossoming and others of introspection.

Moreover, as we traverse this path, let's not forget the power of gratitude. Each day presents countless blessings, some evident and others hidden. By fostering a heart that recognizes and cherishes these divine gifts, we align closer to God's frequency. A heart that is thankful is more receptive, more attuned to God's gentle nudges and signs.

In essence, the voyage to discern God's calling is layered, intricate, and deeply personal. It's a dance between seeking and being found, between questioning and accepting, between striving and surrendering. As this journey unfolds, let's cherish the in-between moments, the pauses, the silent prayers, and the loud proclamations of faith. For in this dance with the Divine, every step, twist, and turn holds a promise of discovery, growth, and a deeper understanding of our purpose under His vast, starry canvas. Let's embrace it with open arms and trusting hearts, for God's script, written especially for each of us, is nothing short of a masterpiece.

The Journey Brings Recognition

As the chapters of our divinely authored story continue, there's a beautiful paradox we come to recognize: while our journey is uniquely our own, we are never truly alone. God's presence is the constant companion, the gentle guide, the compassionate listener, and the force that propels us forward even in moments of hesitation.

Each encounter, each connection we form with others, bears the fingerprints of the Divine. The stranger who offers a kind word on a challenging day, the friend who stands by us in times of trial, the mentor who illuminates our path with wisdom; they're all instruments in God's orchestra, playing a symphony that resonates with our soul's deepest desires and questions.

In the stillness of prayer, when we bare our souls and lay out our hopes, fears, and aspirations, there's an underlying realization that we are part of something far greater than ourselves. This interconnected web of existence, where every action and every choice sends ripples across time and space, is orchestrated with precision and purpose by the Grand Designer.

But with the profound comes the mundane, and therein lies another layer of beauty. For God isn't just present in the life-altering decisions and monumental moments. He's there in the everyday—in the warmth of a morning coffee, in the laughter shared with loved ones, in the serenity of a sunset, and in the pages of a book that speaks to your heart. Recognizing God in these seemingly small moments is a testament to the depth of our relationship with Him.

As the journey continues, it becomes evident that God's calling isn't a one-time revelation, but a continuous evolution. It's a dialogue that evolves as we grow, learn, and experience. While the essence of our purpose remains steadfast, the ways in which we fulfill it expand, transform, and diversify, mirroring our own personal growth and the ever-changing world around us.

Remember, our story, while divinely inspired, is also co-authored by us. God provides the ink and the broad strokes, but the details, the nuances, the colors we bring in, are ours to choose. So, let's wield our pen with courage, faith, and integrity, knowing that with God as our co-writer, our narrative will be one of hope, love, and purposeful living.

As we turn the pages, with anticipation and trust, let's remain anchored in the belief that the best chapters, the most enlightening revelations, and the most profound connections are still ahead of us. With God's grace and guidance, our story is bound to be an epic of spiritual discovery and fulfillment.

Step One
The Profound Shift
Surrender to the Divine Compass

13

As you've journeyed through the initial chapters in Part One of this book, you've embarked on a transformative odyssey. From the pages of Part Two, a powerful pattern has emerged—your life's blueprint in seven steps—leading you towards a life imbued with purpose and resounding with God's glory. Now, as we pause and take a breath, let's retrace our steps and distill the essence of this spiritual pilgrimage.

These seven steps aren't just theories sketched on paper. They are the heartbeat of my personal voyage, the compass that guided my way, and the landmarks that marked my evolution. And if someone had whispered to me years ago where this path would lead, I would've met their words with disbelief. Yet, here I am, a living testament to the wondrous ways God moves in our lives.

Join me as we revisit these transformative steps, understanding their profound impact and seeing how they can be the key to unlocking the secret of God's grand design for you.

Surrendering to the Divine Compass

The year 2016 bore witness to a transformative moment in my life. Standing at the precipice of despair, with a myriad of emotions swirling within, I took a profound leap of faith. Without a map of what lay ahead, I handed over the reins of my journey to the most capable navigator, God. This act of surrender, a deep and heartfelt communion with the Divine, wasn't just a fleeting sentiment; it was the dawn of a reinvigorated life journey, one that would be marked by discovery, faith, and an unwavering pursuit of God's plan.

The words from Philippians echoed in my heart:

"Rejoice in the Lord always; again I will say, rejoice. Let your reasonableness be known to everyone. The Lord is at hand; do not be anxious about anything, but in everything by prayer and supplication with thanksgiving let your requests be made known to God" (Philippians 4:4–6).

Two significant revelations emerged from this initial step of surrender. Firstly, every time I aligned my actions and thoughts with God's divine plan, serendipity played its part. Doors opened, paths cleared, and a deep-seated calmness enveloped me, affirming that I was on the right trajectory. Conversely, whenever I veered off course, surrendering to complacency or distractions, a familiar turbulence returned, manifesting as anxiety and restlessness.

It's rather humbling to admit that it took me over half a century, peppered with both soaring highs and challenging lows, to truly grasp this. I had achieved so much, yet, time and again, I found myself colliding with invisible barriers.

But as I delved deeper into my newfound connection with God, revelations flowed. My directions were clear: move away from the familiar confines of California. Venture into the picturesque landscapes of Idaho. Set roots in the charming town of Coeur d'Alene. With every revelation, a surge of exhilaration coursed through me. What was once mundane suddenly brimmed with possibility. The horizon beckoned with adventures, and every sunrise held the promise of something wondrous.

It's astounding how a singular act of surrender to God's will could pivot my life's narrative so dramatically. Every day bore the question, when would the next chapter in Coeur d'Alene begin? But I had learned to be patient, to wait, to listen and to trust. For I knew, every answer would unfurl in God's impeccable timing, painting my story with hues of grace and purpose.

The First Step to Unveiling Your Destiny: Surrender to God's Will

Ah, the quest for purpose—it's an age-old journey that every soul undertakes. Many of us wander through life, seeking a sign, a compass, something to guide us towards our destiny. We are all in search of that magical blueprint which promises a life of fulfillment and purpose.

Well, dear reader, the treasure map you've been searching for might be closer than you think.

God, in His infinite wisdom and love, has bequeathed to us a manual, a guidebook—the Bible. Through its pages, He whispers secrets, reveals truths, and lays out a roadmap for us. My personal odyssey has been a testimony to this. I've stumbled, faltered, and faced innumerable crossroads. Yet, every lesson, every revelation that life has offered me, has been a gentle nudge from the divine, guiding me back to His Word.

Now, I won't pretend to be an oracle with all the answers. Far from it. But what I can offer you is a compass pointing to the ultimate source of wisdom. To live a life brimming with passion and purpose, we must immerse ourselves in the life and teachings of Jesus Christ. After all, if we are crafted in His image, shouldn't we strive to mirror His grace, strength, and compassion?

Take a moment to reflect on these profound words from the Bible:

"In all your endeavors, recognize Him, and He will illuminate your journey" (Proverbs 3:6).

These words aren't mere poetic phrases. They are a promise that when we put God at the helm, He will steer us through life's tumultuous waters.

Or consider this comforting assurance:

"God hasn't instilled in us a spirit of trepidation; but of vigor, affection, and clarity of thought" (2 Timothy 1:7).

In moments of doubt, when shadows of fear loom large, remember that God has equipped us with a resilient spirit, filled of love and unwavering resolve.

The scriptures also lovingly advises:

"Position yourself humbly before the Lord, and watch as He elevates you to greater heights" (James 4:10).

It's a poignant reminder that in humility, we find our true strength.

But here's the catch—many of us wait for the "perfect" moment to embrace God's plan. We tell ourselves, "Once I secure my finances, once I have a stable family, once all the pieces of my life neatly fall into place; then I'll fully commit to God's path." But, dear friends, faith doesn't work on our timetable. God doesn't call the equipped; He equips the called.

Walking in faith is a leap into the unknown. It's venturing out with trembling hands, a racing heart, and a torrent of doubts, but taking the step anyway, trusting that the Lord is right there, holding our hand. It's saying, "It's just You and me, Lord. Guide me."

Your destiny awaits. Are you ready to surrender to His will and embark on the most extraordinary journey of your life?

Surrender Isn't a One Time Act

The beauty of surrendering to God's will is that it's not a one-time act. But a daily commitment. Each sunrise brings with it an invitation to trust more deeply, to lean more fully into God's embrace. As we journey through the tapestry of our days—with its interwoven threads of joy, pain, hope, and despair—the act of surrender becomes our anchor, grounding us amidst life's unpredictable tides.

Imagine your life as a ship. Many of us often insist on being the captain, navigating through the waters with our limited knowledge and understanding. We rely on our flawed compasses, only to find ourselves lost amidst life's vast ocean. But what if we allowed the divine Captain, with His unfailing compass—the Bible—to guide us? Then, even when storms arise, we'd have the assurance that our ship is being steered by the One who commands the winds and waves.

The Bible is replete with tales of individuals who dared to surrender completely. Consider Abraham, who was willing to sacrifice his son Isaac, trusting God's plan even when it seemed unfathomable. Or Mary, a young woman who accepted the Divine calling to be the mother of Jesus, despite the potential ridicule and ostracism. Their stories are testaments to the boundless blessings and miracles that unfold when we align our will with God's.

Yet, surrender doesn't mean passive resignation. It means actively seeking God's guidance in all aspects of our lives—our relationships, careers, dreams, and even our challenges. It's about dialoguing with Him, seeking His counsel in our decisions, and allowing His wisdom to permeate our thoughts and actions.

Interestingly, many of us often equate surrender with loss—a loss of control, autonomy, or freedom. But in the divine paradox, true freedom is found in surrender. When we let go of our tight grip on life, when we stop trying to control every outcome, we discover a liberating truth: that in God's hands, our lives transform into a masterpiece, more beautiful and purposeful than anything we could have orchestrated on our own.

And so, as you stand at the crossroads of your journey, I invite you: lay down your burdens, your fears, your anxieties. Hand over the reins of your life to the divine Maestro. Trust in His symphony, His timing, His plan. Let the echoes of Proverbs 3:6 reverberate in your heart: "In all your ways acknowledge Him, and He shall direct your paths."

Your adventure with God is just beginning. With every act of surrender, with every step taken in faith, you're not only drawing closer to your divine purpose but also becoming a beacon of hope and inspiration for others to discover their own God-ordained destinies. So, go forth with courage and let your life's symphony play out in perfect harmony with His grand design.

Surrender Isn't About Lack

Remember, surrender is not about giving up or losing, but rather about gaining an infinite source of strength, guidance, and prosperity. As you learn to surrender, you'll find yourself more in tune with the rhythmic dance of life. You'll experience moments of unparalleled clarity, where the noise of the world fades and you can hear God's whispers more distinctly. This journey isn't one of walking blindly, but of following a path illuminated by divine light.

Each of us has a unique story, a personal narrative that intertwines with the larger tapestry of creation. By surrendering, we're not erasing our story, but allowing it to be enriched and redirected by a higher purpose. We become co-authors with God, writing chapters filled with grace, love, and transformation.

Think of Peter, the apostle. Initially, he was a mere fisherman, content with the simplicity of his life. But when he surrendered to Jesus, he transformed into one of the boldest apostles, spreading the gospel far and wide. His surrender didn't diminish his story; it elevated it. Similarly, when you align your narrative with God's purpose, you'll find your role in the grander scheme of things becoming more profound and impactful.

It's also essential to recognize that surrendering is a journey and not a destination. There will be days of unwavering trust, and there will be moments of doubt. And that's okay. Each day offers a fresh start, a new opportunity to realign with God's will. The beauty of faith is that it thrives not in perfection but in persistence.

And while the worldly perspective often equates success with having a plan and being in control, the divine perspective offers a different view. True success, in God's eyes, is the ability to let go, trust, and be led. To acknowledge that while we may have the will, He has the way.

So, dear reader, as you embark on this journey of surrender, remember that you're not alone. Alongside you is a community of believers, each navigating their path, each with their tales of faith and moments of doubt. Share your stories, uplift each other, and let the collective strength propel you forward.

Moreover, let your life be a testimony, a beacon for others still searching for their path. Show them, through your actions and faith, that surrendering to God's will doesn't diminish our lives but elevates them to unparalleled heights. Let the world see that in surrender, there is strength; in faith, there is freedom, and in God, there is an eternal unwavering love.

Step Two
Constant Communion
The Symphony of Prayer and Praise

The journey of faith is a tapestry, woven with threads of divine revelations, and deep-rooted convictions. Central to this tapestry, in my life, is a consistent dialogue with the Creator—a continuous, heart-to-heart conversation with God. It's not merely a ritual; it's a relationship.

Every dawn, I begin with a verbal salutation with raised hands, a heartfelt greeting to the Father, the Son, and the Holy Spirit. These moments are sacred, setting the tone for the day, reminding me of the ever-present Divine embrace. And as twilight heralds the close of the day, I find solace in prayer on my knees. This nightly ritual isn't just about seeking; it's an orchestra of gratitude, recognizing the countless blessings, large and small, that God bestows. Each prayer starts with gratitude, a celebration of God's daily wonders, before delving into the depths of my heart's desires, concerns, and hopes. And as I close, I always affirm my faith with the words: "In the name of Jesus Christ, I pray. Amen. I love you, God! You are my first love!"

Drawing inspiration from Hebrews:

> "By Him therefore let us offer the sacrifice of praise to God continually, that is, the fruit of our lips giving thanks to His name" (Hebrews 13:15).

Again, drawing inspiration from Hebrews 13:15, my journey is illuminated by the continuous light of praise. This act isn't just about routine; it's a testament to a truth I've embraced—that God is paramount, deserving of boundless love, trust, and worship. As a believer, every beat of my heart, every thought, every action, seeks to reflect His glory. My commitment to this is reinforced daily, not just through prayer, but also through studying His Word, immersing myself in the Bible to discern His divine intentions for me.

Rewinding to 2007, a pivotal chapter in my life unfolds—a profound covenant with God when I stood at the threshold of life and death. In those uncertain moments, God, in His infinite mercy, answered my earnest prayers, granting me more precious time on this earthly realm. Time to witness my young sons flourish, time to serve His greater purpose. (For those curious about this transformative period, I delve deeper into it in my memoir, "The Secrets of Prayer: When Death Knocked at My Door.") It's a testament that continuously fuels my spirit of praise. And today, anchored in this gratitude, I revel in a harmonious relationship with our Lord Jesus Christ, a serene fellowship that fills every day with divine peace and purpose.

The Second Step to Unveiling Your Destiny: Pray and Praise God

Imagine a beautiful orchestra playing, each instrument harmonizing with the others, creating a melody so profound and moving that it touches the very core of your being. This symphony is much like our relationship with God, a harmonious dance of prayer and praise that connects our souls with the divine. But, instead of instruments, our tools are our voices, our hearts, and our spirits.

Each morning, as the sun peeks through the horizon, heralding a new day, many of us begin with a prayer, a conversation with our Creator. Just like I harness the serenity from Hillsong's Christian Music Group CDs to center myself, you too can find a method or ritual that connects you to God. And why? Because our hearts understand the profound impact of starting the day by acknowledging His presence. It's a gentle reminder that while the world is vast and can sometimes be overwhelming, we're never alone on this journey.

But it's essential not only to speak but also to listen. Prayer isn't just about asking; it's also about understanding, reflecting, and internalizing. It's a two-way dialogue where we present our hopes, fears, dreams, and anxieties and then pause to listen to the gentle whispers or roaring affirmations God sends our way.

And as you go through your day, remember that every moment is an opportunity to commune with God. The beauty of our relationship with Him is that it doesn't need a grand gesture or a specific setting. Whether you're amidst nature marveling at His creation, or in a bustling city observing the intricate tapestry of human life, you can always turn your thoughts upwards.

Moreover, sprinkled throughout our days should be moments of pure praise. These aren't just reserved for when things go right. Even in trials, there's a reason to celebrate—for growth, for resilience, for the promise of God's unfailing support. As the Bible encourages, we should "Rejoice evermore." For in our joy and gratitude, we align ourselves with the vibrancy of life God intended for us.

And, dear reader, as you walk this path, seeking your tailor-made purpose, always remember the promise in Ephesians 2:10: "You are God's masterpiece, fashioned with care, destined for greatness, and equipped with everything you need to leave a mark on this world." As you embrace the rhythm of prayer and praise, let it be your guiding compass, directing you towards a life overflowing with purpose and passion. Let this symphony play loudly in your life, so much so that others can't help but join in, drawn by the captivating melody of a life in tune with God.

A Deep Dive Into the Heart

Just as ripples spread out when a single pebble is dropped into the water, the impact of your daily communion with God can have far-reaching effects, not just for you, but for those around you. Every individual you come across in your journey, every interaction you have, becomes an opportunity to radiate the divine love and understanding you've garnered.

There's a popular saying that actions speak louder than words. In the realm of faith, this couldn't be truer. Each of us has been uniquely designed by God, with distinct talents, gifts, and passions. But what ties us all together is the inherent desire to belong, to understand our place in this vast universe, and to find meaning in our existence. And that's where your role becomes pivotal.

Sharing your faith journey isn't just about speaking of God's wonders, although that is essential. It's about exemplifying a Christ-like attitude in every facet of life, showing compassion to the weary, understanding to the lost, and love to the forsaken. This lived testimony has the power to touch hearts in ways mere words might not.

Additionally, taking time for personal reflection is paramount. The world we live in is noisy, filled with distractions that can sometimes make it hard to hear God's voice. But by regularly diving deep into the Scriptures, meditating on His promises, and actively seeking His guidance, you fine-tune your spiritual senses. You begin to discern His voice amidst the chaos, guiding you, comforting you, and reminding you of your divine purpose.

Remember, your journey of faith is not a solitary one. While you have the Holy Spirit as your constant companion, you also have a community of believers. Engage with them, share your insights, listen to theirs, and grow together. There's strength in unity, and as the body of Christ, when one succeeds, we all do.

Finally, always carry with you the essence of 1 Thessalonians 5:16–18: "In the highs and lows, in certainty and doubt, in joy and sorrow, let your heart continuously be in a state of gratitude, for that's where true contentment lies." As you foster this daily rhythm of prayer and praise, you not only draw closer to God but also inspire others to embark on this transformative journey. Let your life be the beacon, a shining testament to God's endless love and grace.

Bridging the Gap
Between the Divine and Daily Life

It's intriguing how the subtle moments of silent reflection can create a symphony of transformation. This melody, born from the heart's deepest chambers, connects us to the divine, resonating with a frequency that harmonizes our soul with the Creator's intent. But how do we sustain this symphony amidst life's cacophony?

For many, the challenge is integrating spiritual practices into their daily grind. Life has a rhythm, a pace, and sometimes it feels like a sprint. But your spiritual journey, much like a symphony, requires various tempos—sometimes allegro, sometimes adagio. And it's essential to honor each pace.

Prayer isn't merely a ritual; it's a relationship. It's a conversation with God, where you're both speaking and listening. It's where burdens are shared, and blessings are acknowledged. But much like any relationship, it requires effort. Setting aside time each day, perhaps during those quiet morning moments or the tranquil hours of the evening, ensures this relationship thrives.

Moreover, it's not just about secluded moments with God. Transform your daily tasks into acts of worship. As you write, visualize each word as a prayer. As you interact with others, see each conversation as an opportunity to spread love. And as you face challenges, view them as lessons designed to mold and refine you.

There's a profound power in gratitude. It shifts perspectives, turning what we have into enough. Remembering to give thanks daily, for both small and grand blessings, helps ground you. It serves as a reminder of God's constant presence and infinite love. When you actively choose gratitude, you're also choosing joy, resilience, and faith.

And as you walk this path, remember you're not alone. Surround yourself with like-minded souls. Join study groups, attend workshops, or simply share a cup of coffee with someone who understands your journey. These connections provide encouragement, wisdom, and the sheer joy of shared experiences.

Embrace the beautiful paradox of faith—it's deeply personal, yet universally binding. As you journey onward, letting the symphony of prayer and praise guide you, you'll find that the divine isn't somewhere out there; it's intricately woven into every moment, every challenge, and every joy of your daily life. And in this realization, you'll discover a purpose that's both profound and beautifully simple.

The Orchestra of Life

Think of life as a vast orchestra, with each instrument representing an aspect of our daily experiences, responsibilities, dreams, and aspirations. Some instruments take the lead, like the grand piano or the powerful brass section. Others provide the harmony, like the soft strings or gentle woodwinds. But in this grand orchestra, there's a conductor—and that conductor is our faith and communion with God.

Each day brings a new score, sometimes challenging, sometimes uplifting, and at other times, a blend of both. It might seem that some instruments are out of tune or that the melody gets lost amidst the clamor. That's when the role of the conductor becomes crucial. Through constant communion, through a dedicated symphony of prayer and praise, you can find the rhythm again, even in the most challenging compositions.

Your morning meditations and prayers playing Hillsong music, perhaps, are like those initial moments when the conductor raises the baton, signaling the orchestra to get ready. It's a sacred time when you align yourself with the divine, seeking guidance, strength, and clarity for the day's performance.

Remember, every instrument, no matter how insignificant it might seem, plays a crucial role in the orchestra. Similarly, every act, thought, and word in your daily life contributes to your purpose. Sometimes you might question the significance of your role, or wonder if your efforts even matter. But here's the beautiful truth—they do. Every small act of kindness, every whispered prayer, every moment of gratitude, adds depth and richness to the symphony of your life.

Just as Ephesians 2:10 highlights, you're divinely crafted. Every talent, skill, passion, or ability you possess has been carefully chosen, "tailor-made" for you, setting the stage for the unique melody you're destined to play.

With every challenge you encounter, imagine it as a complex musical piece. Initially, it may seem overwhelming, perhaps even discordant. But with faith as your guide, with prayer as your constant rhythm, you can navigate through, finding the harmony amidst the chaos.

Concluding on a note from 1 Thessalonians 5:16–18, "rejoice in every note of your life's symphony, pray with fervor and consistency, and in every crescendo or diminuendo, give thanks." This is the will of God, and as you embrace it, your life's music will not only touch your soul but also resonate with countless others, inspiring them to find their divine melody.

Step Three
The Living Word
A Deep Dive into Divine Wisdom

15

Embarking on a spiritual voyage, with the vast oceans of human interpretations and religious doctrines stretching endlessly before me, I made a conscious choice. I chose to steer clear of the noisy shores of man-made beliefs. Instead, I aimed for the pure, untamed waters of divine knowledge, desiring only the unadulterated essence of God's messages in the Holy Scriptures. It wasn't about aligning with a religious denomination or man's philosophical musings; it was about diving deep into the reservoir of the Bible's wisdom, untouched and unchanged.

Drawing inspiration from James:

"But be you doers of the word, and not hearers only, deceiving yourselves" (James 1:22).

Again, drawing inspiration from James, I realized the importance of active engagement with the scriptures. My pursuit wasn't a passive absorption. It became an active quest, involving various tools and resources. Immersing myself in the Bible, study Bibles, probing through extra-biblical books, devouring CDs, DVDs, enlightening videos, and even assimilating insights from selected teachers and guest speakers, I journeyed through a spectrum of biblical understanding. My intense engagement and meticulous note-taking blossomed into my inaugural projects, "Passion for Christ: New Beginnings," "The Living Waters" series, and the "New Narrated Study Bible (NNSB)." To first grasp the overarching narrative of the Bible and then to delve—with a discerning heart—into each of its 66-books, felt nothing short of a spiritual revelation. The mosaics of the scriptures started aligning, offering me a vivid panorama of God's grand design.

And oh, the transformation it ushered in! It wasn't just about acquiring knowledge; it was about internalizing a divine epiphany. Through the verses, chapters, and books, I felt God's voice guiding me, enlightening me, and reshaping my worldview. This deep dive became my life's mission, my divine calling. Welcoming the Lord into my heart's inner sanctum, I witnessed the blossoming of a new realm. A realm where passion for God was the sun that shone brightly, where thinking and speaking became harmonized with Christ's teachings, where I began to see my reflection through Jesus' compassionate eyes. The Holy Spirit, dwelling within me, became my inner compass always guiding me towards choices that resonated with peace.

As the days turned into weeks, and weeks into months, and years into years, my journey with the Bible started bearing fruits. Miracles, both subtle and profound, began to manifest. Each day, every verse, each prayer became a testament to the transformative power of truly knowing God through His word.

The Third Step to Unveiling Your Destiny: Navigating the Ocean of Divine Wisdom

Imagine for a moment that you're standing on the shores of a vast ocean. The water stretches endlessly, its depths unknown and its horizon distant. This ocean, my dear reader, represents the boundless wisdom contained in the Bible—the Living Word of God. Each ripple, each wave, is a lesson, a parable, a piece of guidance from the divine. And as you stand on that shore, you have the choice to merely admire the view or to dive deep into its depths, seeking the treasures that lie within.

Now, while I stand alongside you, having taken many a dive into this vast ocean, I humbly acknowledge that I am but a fellow explorer, continuously captivated by its richness. Through my life's journey, God's Word has been the compass guiding me, illuminating my path even in the darkest nights. I've gleaned countless lessons, felt His presence in the most unexpected verses, and found solace in His promises. Yet, I remain a student, always eager, always thirsting for more.

The Bible is not just a historical text or a collection of moral teachings. It's a living testament, an ongoing conversation between the Creator and His creation. Every story, every verse, resonates with the timeless truths of human existence, of love, sacrifice, faith, and redemption. Jesus Christ, the embodiment of God's love, lived as one of us, reflecting virtues and character traits that we, being made in His image, are called to emulate.

To truly embrace the life of passion and purpose that you yearn for, delving into the Bible is essential. It's like a treasure map, waiting for eager seekers to uncover its hidden gems. Each reading, each meditation, offers a fresh revelation, a new perspective that aligns you closer with your God-given purpose.

However, as with any journey, it's essential not to tread alone. Surround yourself with a community, be it an online group, a study group, a mentor, or even books and resources that enhance your understanding. Challenge your interpretations, question your beliefs, and let every answer you find draw you closer to Him.

Lastly, as you set forth on this spiritual voyage, always remember that the journey is as significant as the destination. The Bible is not just to be read but to be lived. Let its teachings seep into your daily actions, let its wisdom guide your decisions, and let its promises uplift your spirit. In doing so, you'll find that the Living Word becomes a part of you, guiding, nurturing, and transforming you into the best version of yourself.

The Bible Is Also Called the Will of God

In the vast tapestry of life, where countless threads of experiences, emotions, and encounters intertwine, the Bible—also called the Will of God—stands as a golden thread, weaving purpose, direction, and meaning into every aspect. The Living Word, with its profound narratives and timeless truths, doesn't merely offer black and white instructions but paints a vibrant, multi-hued canvas for us to interpret, understand, and most importantly, internalize.

Imagine the Bible as a deep well, filled with the purest water. Each time you draw from it, you're not just quenching a physical thirst but nourishing your very soul. It's a reservoir of insights, offering clarity in confusion, strength in weakness, and hope in despair. As you immerse yourself deeper into its verses, you'll find layers of understanding unfurling, like petals of a blooming rose.

The characters in the Bible, from the courageous David to the persevering Job, from the faithful Ruth to the visionary Isaiah, aren't merely figures from the past. They are mirrors reflecting our own challenges, doubts, joys, and aspirations. Their stories resonate because, at their core, they grapple with the same human experiences we do. By studying their lives, their choices, and their faith, we get a roadmap for our own journey.

Yet, it's essential to approach the Bible not just as a reader but as a seeker. A seeker who's open to being challenged, who's willing to wrestle with the tough questions, and who's eager to embrace the transformative power of the Word. There's an ancient saying, "When the student is ready, the teacher will appear." In many ways, the Bible is that eternal teacher, always ready to guide, but awaiting our genuine, inquisitive, and open-hearted approach.

Moreover, the Living Word is a dynamic evolving with you as you journey through different seasons of life. The verse that offered comfort during a time of loss might inspire courage in the face of a new challenge. The parable that once seemed puzzling might suddenly shine with clarity in light of a personal experience. It's a testament to the Bible's enduring relevance and its ability to speak to us in myriad ways.

In your quest for purpose and passion, let the Living Word be your anchor. Let it be the gentle whisper that guides you in silent moments, the triumphant shout that celebrates your victories, and the comforting embrace that holds you during storms. As you navigate the complexities of life, remember that in the pages of the Bible lies the wisdom of the ages, waiting to be discovered, cherished, and lived.

The Bible Isn't a Static Document

The beauty of the Bible is that it's not a static document confined to a particular time or place, it's a living conversation between God and humanity, an invitation to engage, question, and grow. Each time you revisit a passage, it might whisper a different message, offer a fresh perspective, or provide a new insight, relevant to your current situation.

Diving into the Bible is akin to diving into an ocean. On the surface, you see the waves and the reflection of the sky. But as you go deeper, you begin to discover the colorful corals, the intriguing marine life, and the treasures hidden in its depths. Similarly, a cursory reading of the Bible might give you an overview of its stories and teachings. Still, a deep, contemplative dive reveals the profound wisdom, intricate patterns, and divine messages embedded within.

One might wonder, why is it essential to go beyond the surface? The world today is filled with noise—information overload, constant notifications, and the hustle to keep up. In this cacophony, the soul often seeks solace, a voice of reason, and a beacon of hope. The Bible, with its timeless teachings, offers precisely that. However, to extract its nectar, one must be willing to spend time, reflect, and meditate on its words.

To truly internalize the Living Word, consider adopting the practice of "lectio Divina," an ancient Christian tradition that involves reading, meditation, prayer, and contemplation. It's not about how many verses or chapters you cover, but the depth with which you engage with them.

- **Reading (Lectio)**. Slowly read a chosen passage, savoring each word and phrase.

- **Meditation (Meditation)**. Reflect on the text, asking, "What does this passage say to me?"

- **Prayer (Oratio)**. Respond to God based on your meditation. Share your feelings, desires, questions, and seek guidance.

- **Contemplation (Contemplatio)**. Rest in God's presence, allowing His word to permeate your being, transforming you from within.

Imagine a world where, before making decisions or confronting challenges, we turned to the Bible for guidance. Where, instead of seeking validation from the world, we sought affirmation from the Word. The profound wisdom it offers isn't merely for personal growth but can be the catalyst for positive change in our communities and the world at large.

In your journey of discovery, let the Bible be more than just a book. Let it be a companion, a mentor, a guide. As you walk the path of life, hand in hand with the Living Word, you'll find that the divine wisdom it offers illuminates every step, making the journey as beautiful as the destination.

God, The Answer to Every Problem

Let's think of life as a grand, intricate tapestry. Each thread in this tapestry represents a lesson, an experience, a challenge, or a blessing. Now, imagine if you had a guide, a handbook of sorts, that provided insights, directions, and sometimes even solutions to the patterns and designs life weaves. This is the magic the Bible brings into our lives.

But to fully embrace its magic, one must be willing to immerse themselves in its teachings, constantly seeking the divine wisdom concealed within its verses.

Consider this: In our fast-paced world, where instant gratification is the norm, and digital devices are an extension of ourselves, we seldom pause. We seldom reflect. But the Bible demands both patience and reflection. It's not a quick fix, but a life-long commitment to understanding God's Word and finding its relevance in our modern lives.

There's a saying that when you read a good book, you want to tell someone about it. With the Bible, it's a tad different. When you truly understand and feel its teachings, you want to live by it and inspire others to do the same. It becomes a part of your being, influencing your choices and guiding your path.

The Living Word isn't merely about reading scriptures. It's about absorbing them, wrestling with them, questioning them, and eventually, embodying them. Each story, each parable, each lesson from the Bible has multiple layers. The story of David isn't just about defeating Goliath; it's about faith, courage, and the idea that with God on our side, no challenge is too big. The tale of the prodigal son isn't just about a boy who lost his way; it's about redemption, forgiveness, and the unconditional love of the Father.

So, as you take this deep dive, think of it as an exploration. Explore not just the words written but the spaces between them. Seek not just the stories told, but the lessons they impart. Dive deep, not to merely swim in the waters of divine wisdom but to become one with them.

In this journey with the Living Word, you won't just be reading about miracles; you'll be living them. You won't just learn about God's love; you'll feel it enveloping you. And as you transform, you become a beacon of hope, light, and inspiration for others, guiding them towards the path of righteousness and divine purpose.

God Speaks In a Small Voice

And there lies the transformative power of the Living Word: it's not a passive read, but an active engagement. One doesn't just read the Bible; one experiences it. Through its teachings, we begin to perceive the world differently. It's like donning a new pair of glasses that allows us to view life from a divine perspective. Our problems don't disappear, but our capacity to handle them, understand them, and learn from them magnifies exponentially.

Remember, God's wisdom doesn't shout; it whispers. In the quiet moments of reflection, in the silent prayers at dawn, in the hushed conversations with your inner self, the Bible communicates. These moments of connection, where we are synced with the divine, are truly euphoric. It's like the universe itself is revealing its secrets, one verse at a time.

However, diving deep into the Bible is not always an easy journey. There will be passages that challenge your existing beliefs, verses that seem perplexing, and teachings that demand unwavering faith. But that's the beauty of it. The Bible is not meant to be a comfort book; it's a growth book. It pushes, prods, and prompts you to evolve, to rise above the mundane, and to achieve spiritual ascension.

Engaging with the Living Word is like embarking on a quest. Along the way, you'll encounter moments of enlightenment, phases of doubt, stretches of contemplation, and periods of sheer joy. But with each step, with each chapter, with each verse, you inch closer to the divine, closer to your true purpose, closer to the very essence of existence.

One might wonder, "How does a book, written thousands of years ago, hold relevance in our contemporary world?" That's the miracle of the Bible. Its teachings are timeless. Its lessons are universal. Its stories resonate with every heart, every soul, across time and space.

So, dear reader, as you delve deeper into the Living Word, remember that you're not just learning about God's plan; you're a part of it. Each verse you internalize, each teaching you embody, each act of kindness you perform, contributes to this grand cosmic design. Your life, with its joys, sorrows, victories, and challenges, becomes a testament to God's everlasting love and wisdom. Embrace the journey, cherish the revelations, and let the Bible be the compass that guides you to your true north.

Step Four
Dancing to the Divine Symphony
Embracing God's Guided Path

In the vast tapestry of life, threads of decisions, actions, and consequences entwine. As I journeyed through this intricate design, I realized a fundamental truth: surrendering to God's will transformed those threads into a harmonious pattern, leading me to an authentic and fulfilled life.

The scriptures, a reservoir of wisdom . . .

"For the flesh desires what is contrary to the Spirit, and the Spirit what is contrary to the flesh. They are in conflict with each other so that you do not do whatever you want" (Galatians 5:17).

The scriptures, a reservoir of wisdom, remind us of the eternal battle within. It presents a dauting list of transgressions, from adultery and idolatry to envy and revelries, all of which distance us from inheriting God's Kingdom.

But since that pivotal moment in 2016, a paradigm shift occurred in my heart. I decided to place God at the helm of my life, allowing His directions to steer my path. And oh, what a wondrous journey it has been! By sidelining my own desires and letting God's blueprint guide me, I found my world overflowing with blessings, joy, and contentment.

The journey wasn't an overnight metamorphosis. It took years, each day a chapter, each moment a verse, culminating in the story you're reading now. By November 2018, God's voice became unmistakable. He beckoned me back to the world of publishing, not just as a means of livelihood but as a divine mission. Thus were born The Ridge Publishing Group, its imprints Guardians of Biblical Truth, the New Narrated Study Bible (NNSB); my personal authorial ventures under LAMoeszinger.com, and the Urban Chronicles Publishing House. The trail didn't stop there. AuthorsDoor Group, the AuthorsDoor Leadership programs, Defending the Faith documentaries in print, and innovative board games and card games came into existence.

You might wonder, why such an expansive portfolio? Every venture, every creation, was a medium through which I shared my discoveries and insights about God and the scriptures. It's a cycle: the more I learn, the more I feel compelled to share, and the more I share, the deeper my understanding becomes. I've always been voracious for information, and in this spiritual journey, I realized that this innate curiosity wasn't a mere quirk. It was a divine calling.

How can I assert this with such conviction? Because every step taken in faith has been rewarded with blessings that often defy comprehension. When I entrusted my path to God, pleading with Him to let me nurture my sons, I made a pact. I might not always decipher His plans perfectly, but my faith would remain unwavering. As you read this, know that my journey is testament to the miracles that unfold when we walk hand in hand with faith, letting God lead the dance.

The Fourth Step to Unveiling Your Destiny: Navigating Life with God as the Conductor

Imagine, if you will, life as a grand ballroom. The music begins, an enchanting melody that resonates deep within your soul. You find yourself in the middle, unsure, hesitating. It's the symphony of existence, of choices and decisions, playing around you. But what if I told you that you weren't meant to dance this waltz of life alone? There's a divine choreographer, a heavenly guide, waiting to lead you—and His name is God.

"Many are the plans in a person's heart, but it is the Lord's purpose that prevails" (Proverbs 19:21).

It's a comforting thought, isn't it? That amid the noise and chaos of life, there is a purpose, a divine script, already written for us. It's like finding out there's a map for an intricate maze you're navigating. But just having the map isn't enough. It requires trust—faith in a plan we might not always see or understand.

However, the distractions are plenty. Our world often seduces us with glittering temptations—fleeting moments of pleasure, the insatiable desire for material wealth, and the transient highs of power and pride. Yet, deep down, there's an innate understanding that these are but ephemeral. They dazzle, they shine, but like the fleeting notes of a song, they soon fade away.

"For all that is in the world—the desires of the flesh and the desires of the eyes and pride in possessions—is not from the Father but is from the world. And the world is passing away along with its desires, but whoever does the will of God abides forever" (1 John 13:20–21).

It's easy to lose oneself in the frantic tempo of modern life. The next big purchase, the next achievement, the constant comparison with others. But when we stop, even for a moment, and introspect, we realize the hollowness of such pursuits. On the final day, when the music stops, what remains? It's not our possessions but the memories we made, the lives we touched, the legacy of love and kindness we leave behind.

"But seek first the kingdom of God and his righteousness, and all these things will be added to you" (Matthew 6:33).

The path to a purpose-driven life isn't about abandoning the world but redefining our relationship with it. It's about aligning our desires with God's will, treating every challenge as a lesson, every setback as a stepping stone, and every success as a testament to His grace.

In the Epistle of James, we are reminded:

"Submit yourselves therefore to God. Resist the devil, and he will flee from you" (James 4:7).

This verse encapsulates the core of our journey—a surrender to the divine, a will to walk the righteous path, and the unwavering belief that when we dance in sync with the divine symphony, with God leading our steps, we are truly unstoppable. So, dear reader, put on your dancing shoes, let go of your fears, and let God lead you in this wondrous waltz of life.

Harmonizing with the Heavenly Beat: The Joy of Following God's Rhythm

As we continue our dance, there's an element that's absolutely crucial to mastering this divine choreography: Trust. This trust is not just in God's existence but in His wisdom, His timing, and His infinite love for us. We might stumble, take a misstep, or even lose our rhythm, but with every misadventure, there's a loving hand reaching out, steadying us, and guiding us back to the dance floor.

> "Trust in the Lord with all your heart and lean not on your own understanding; in all your ways submit to Him, and He will make your paths straight" (Proverbs 3:5–6).

The dance floor of life is fraught with challenges, with tests of faith, but these aren't designed to push us away; they're there to pull us closer to God. When we trust in Him wholly, shedding our apprehensions, we start dancing with grace, fluidity, and with joy that emanates from the very core of our being.

And here's the thing: our dance is unique. It's a testament to our individual journey, our personal relationship with God. It isn't about perfection. But about progress, not about the steps we get right, but the spirit with which we dance.

149

However, the divine dance isn't a solo performance. It's a collaborative effort, a group dance. We aren't alone on this floor. Our fellow dancers—our family, friends, and even strangers—are on similar journeys. Some might be waltzing gracefully, others might be learning the steps, but everyone is an essential part of this grand choreography. Our role, in addition to mastering your steps, is to uplift others, guide the ones who falter, and celebrate the ones who excel.

"Therefore encourage one another and build each other up, just as in fact you are doing" (1 Thessalonians 5:11).

Lastly, remember, our dance with God isn't about reaching a destination. It's about cherishing the journey, relishing every moment, every step, every turn. The music will have its highs and lows, crescendos and decrescendos, but through it all, we must keep dancing, keep believing, and most importantly, keep surrendering to the maestro, our God. For in surrender, we find freedom; in trust, we find joy; and in dance, we find purpose. So, embrace the rhythm, surrender to the flow, and let God's divine symphony guide your soul!

The Steps of Surrender and Sync: Discovering Your Spiritual Groove

When we think of dancing, we often imagine a choreographed series of steps. However, this spiritual dance with God isn't about prescribed movements, but about attuning our hearts and souls to the divine rhythm and letting that guide our steps.

As the music of God's purpose unfolds, it's like a song that speaks directly to the soul. Every note resonates, every beat beckons. We're not just passive listeners; we're active participants, with the opportunity to make the song our own, in harmony with God's intentions.

"Let the word of Christ dwell in you richly, teaching and admonishing one another in all wisdom, singing psalms and hymns and spiritual songs, with thankfulness in your hearts to God" (Colossians 3:16).

1. **Start with an Open Heart**. The first step to dance with God is to approach Him with an open heart, ready to receive, ready to learn, and most importantly, ready to trust.

2. **Listen Intently**. Pay close attention to the whispers of the Holy Spirit. Often, the cues for our next step in the dance come as a gentle nudge, a soft push, or an inner feeling.

3. **Embrace the Unexpected**. There will be times when God leads you in directions you hadn't imagined. Instead of resisting, surrender and trust the choreographer of our lives. He sees the bigger picture and knows where each turn and twist will lead.

4. **Dance for an Audience of One**. While others are watching, remember your primary purpose is to be in sync with God. Seeking validation from the world can often disrupt our rhythm.

   "Whatever you do, work heartily, as for the Lord and not for men" (Colossians 3:23).

5. **Find Your Unique Style**. God has bestowed upon each of us unique gifts and talents. Discover yours and use them to glorify Him in your dance. Let your dance be a reflection of your personal relationship with God.

6. **Offer a Helping Hand**. As you get comfortable with your dance, reach out to those struggling with their steps. Guide them, support them, and together find joy in this divine journey.

"Bear one another's burdens, and so fulfill the law of Christ" (Galatians 6:2).

In the end, dancing to the divine symphony isn't about perfection but perseverance. It's about the moments of pure joy when you're in complete alignment with God, and it's also about the lessons learned when you miss a step or two.

Always remember, in this dance of life, you're never alone. God is your partner, leading you, guiding you, and celebrating with you with every step you take. So, let go of inhibitions, dive deep into the rhythm, and let your soul dance in the splendor of God's love!

The Graceful Waltz of Faith and Trust

In our dance with the Divine, there's an undeniable magic that happens when we're in tune with God's frequency. It's like being in a ballroom, where every step, every twirl, and every leap is in harmony with God's melody. Here's how you can maintain that connection and make your dance one of utter joy and surrender:

1. **Stay Rooted in His Word**. The Bible is not just a collection of ancient texts; it's a dynamic playbook for our dance. Dive into it regularly, allowing scriptures to guide your movements and decisions.

"Your word is a lamp to my feet and a light to my path" (Psalm 119:105).

2. **Embrace Growth**. Sometimes, the dance may challenge you, pushing you out of your comfort zone. Remember, these moments are God's way of making you a more versatile dancer, capable of bigger and grander performances.

3. **Maintain a Heart of Gratitude**. Even if you stumble, always come back to a place of thankfulness. Recognize the beauty in every step, the growth in every misstep, and the love that surrounds you.

   "Give thanks in all circumstances; for this is God's will for you in Christ Jesus" (1 Thessalonians 5:18).

4. **Celebrate Every Victory**. Whether it's mastering a complex routine or simply taking a step after a long pause, rejoice in every milestone. Share your joy with others, allowing them to be inspired by your journey.

5. **Learn from Fellow Dancers**. Just as in a dance class, observing others can give you new perspectives and techniques. Surround yourself with those who uplift you, challenge you, and push you to new heights.

   "As iron sharpens iron, so one person sharpens another" (Proverbs 27:17).

6. **Continuously Seek His Guidance**. The dance never truly ends. As you journey through life, always keep an open channel with God. Let Him know your desires, your fears, and seek His wisdom at every juncture.

   "Ask, and it will be given to you; seek, and you will find; knock, and the door will be opened to you" (Matthew 7:7).

In the end, dancing to God's symphony is a choice—a decision to live with purpose, passion, and unyielding faith. As you surrender to His will, every move becomes a testament to His grace, every twirl a celebration of His love. So, put on your dancing shoes, let your heart be light, and let every step you take be a beautiful testament to the profound love and guidance of our Divine Choreographer.

Step Five
Embracing God's Promises
A Testament to Unwavering Faith

17

November 2018—A month and a year etched in gold in the chronicles of my life. As I reflected on the years that had rolled by, I realized God had been orchestrating a divine symphony, leading me to a grand crescendo. Between the transformative years of 2016 to 2018, my fidelity to God's grand design bore fruits beyond my wildest dreams. My life, once filled with obstacles and challenges, now resonated with tranquility. The cacophony had been replaced by a harmonious melody, and it was just me, my loving husband, and our two loyal canine companions in a haven that felt like paradise. Amidst this serenity, clarity dawned upon me, and I recognized the path God had meticulously laid out for me.

Echoing through time and space, the words from Isaiah offered solace and strength . . .

"Fear not, for I am with you; be not dismayed, for I am your God. I will strengthen you, yes, I will help you, I will uphold you with My righteous right hand" (Isaiah 41:10).

Such promises serve as luminous beacons, guiding Christians through stormy seas and dark nights.

The journey of a Christian is not one paved with roses. Like any intrepid traveler, I too faced my share of tempests. During moments of despair, I realized my gaze had shifted from the eternal beacon, God, and was lost in the fleeting shadows of the world. My heart weighed down with melancholy, I turned to prayer. In 2007, and again in 2016, my soul reached out to the divine, seeking solace and guidance. Those were the moments when my commitment to God deepened, becoming as unbreakable as a diamond.

The secret to navigating life's tumultuous waters lies in anchoring oneself to the unwavering promises of God. In doing so, the mind finds its sanctuary, a haven of peace amidst chaos. The old version of me, shackled by worldly desires and fears, had to wither away, making room for a renewed, spiritual self. This rebirth, a metamorphosis, was my key to transcend the mundane and embrace the divine promises of God. Every challenge, every setback, became a stepping stone, leading me to a higher realm of understanding and faith. And in that sanctified space, I found my true calling, purpose, and destiny, forever intertwined with the love and guidance of the Almighty.

The Fifth Step to Unveiling Your Destiny: A Testament to Unwavering Faith

In the journey to surrendering to God's blueprint for our lives, we arrive at a pivotal milestone—embracing God's promises. This step is a testament to unwavering faith, a commitment to trust in the celestial vows that have been whispered through the ages. It's about finding that sacred space where our career and faith align, guided by the divine foresight that is promised to us.

Let's immerse ourselves in the depth of Jeremiah 29:11, where we find the promise of a future crafted by the divine hand itself. This isn't a vague hope but a tailored assurance. Our professional aspirations are not just ours alone; they're interwoven with the grand tapestry that God has envisioned. Here lies the bold affirmation that our pursuits are not in vain—the meetings, the projections, the deadlines all serve a greater good that we may not yet see but can surely believe.

> "For I know the plans I have for you, declares the Lord, plans for welfare and not for evil, to give you a future and a hope" (Jeremiah 29:11).

Imagine this promise as a river of peace running through the chaos of your workday. When disappointment looms or success feels just out of reach, envision yourself as part of a divine narrative where every setback is a setup for a comeback authored by God.

Then there's the melody of Romans 8:28–29, which resonates with the truth that in all things, God works for our good. The harmony of these words with our career is profound. They remind us that our vocation is more than a job—it's a calling, a part of the puzzle that is being pieced together by the Almighty. Each task, each role we undertake is a step towards being shaped into the likeness of His Son, our ultimate calling.

> "And we know for those who love God all things work together for good, for those who are called according to His purpose. For those whom He foreknew He also predestined to be conformed to the image of His Son, in order that He might be the firstborn among many brothers" (Romans 8:28–29).

Carry this melody in your heart as you navigate the workplace. Let it be the soundtrack to your career decisions, the background music that calms your anxious thoughts, and the tune that you hum as you work towards your goals knowing that they align with something far greater.

And in the glow of James 1:17, we are reminded that every good and perfect gift descends from the Father. Our talents and skills are not random; they are bestowed upon us for a purpose. They are the tools we are given to construct a life that mirrors the heavenly blueprint. Our careers, then, become an expression of these gifts, a showcase of the divine generosity that is constant and unwavering.

> "Every good gift and every perfect gift is from above, coming down from the Father of lights, with whom there is no variation or shadow due to change" (James 1:17).

Let this truth light up your workplace as a constant reminder. Let it be the motivation behind your work ethic, the inspiration for your creativity, and the reason you approach each task with integrity and excellence.

To live out this step, take these scriptures and let them be the bedrock of your daily professional life. Meditate on them as you prepare for your day, let them guide your decisions and interactions, and return to them when the road seems unclear. They are not just words; they are the compass that can guide you to your divine destiny.

By embracing God's promises, we do not just read them; we let them take root in our lives. They become our strategy for a faith-aligned career, the blueprint for our life's work, and the assurance that our labor is not in vain but is a part of God's intricate and perfect plan. This step is an invitation to a life of faith, a call to live out the divine promises, and a charge to trust in the path laid out for us—one that leads to a future filled with hope, purpose, and fulfillment.

Embracing God's Promises as Life's True North

Embracing God's promises is about finding and holding onto the celestial coordinates that guide us through life's storms and doldrums alike. It's not just about knowing these promises; it's about letting them take root in our hearts and direct our very steps. Here's how to continue to make God's promises the compass by which you navigate:

- **Engrave Promises on Your Heart**. Just as ancient mariners relied on the stars to navigate the vast oceans, let the promises of God be the celestial points you turn to, both in times of uncertainty and in moments of joy. Internalize these promises by memorizing them, turning them into personal affirmations. Say them out loud, "For I know the plans I have for me, declares the Lord, plans for welfare and not for evil, to give me a future and a hope."

- **Reflect in Prayerful Meditation**. Engage in a daily practice of mediation on these promises. In the quiet corners of your morning or the silent moments before sleep, ponder the depth

159

of God's words. Allow the Holy Spirit to reveal the layers and personal relevance of each promise to your life and circumstances.

- **Promises as Your Decision-Making Framework**. Let these promises guide your choices. When faced with a decision, large or small, ask yourself which option aligns best with the truths you've embraced. Does this path reflect the plans for good and not for disaster, for a future and a hope that He speaks of?

- **Create Visual Symbols**. Move beyond words on a page to tangible symbols. Perhaps a tree to represent growth and life, an anchor for steadfastness, or a light that dispels darkness. These can become powerful visual cures that remind you of God's promises, providing comfort and reassurance when needed.

- **The Shared Journey**. No one walks this path alone. As you embrace God's promises, share them. Our words can offer strength to others. Build a community of believers around you who can hold these promises with you, creating a collective strength that can face any challenge.

- **Living Testimonies**. Remember, you are a living testimony to the faithfulness of God. Your life, transformed by these promises, serves as a beacon to others. Live in such a way that others can see the hope and future God has granted you, inspiring them to seek the same for themselves.

- **The Continual Feast**. Lastly, let the promises of God be a source of continual nourishment. Just as one does not eat once and then never again, so too must we come to God's promises regularly, feasting on His truth to sustain us day by day.

Embracing God's promises is not merely a mental assent to the truths of Scripture. It is a full, living embrace that shapes who we are, the decisions we make, and the way we view our journey through life. It's an active, vibrant process that turns belief into behavior and doctrine into daily living.

Wisdom and Lessons

- **God is Always with Me—I will not fear**—embracing the assurance. Fear operates as a significant hindrance, often leveraged by negative forces to distract and distress us. The illusion that God is distant is a common deception. However, experience and faith teach us that many of our fears are unfounded. By refusing to live in the shadow of "what ifs," we choose to dwell in the light of God's presence, which is a constant reality.

- **God is Always in Control—I will not doubt**—trusting in divine sovereignty. Though the Scriptures might not spell it out verbatim, the narrative of the Bible collectively reassures us of God's unwavering sovereignty. Choosing to submit to His authority is a liberation from the bondage of worldly desires. Recognizing His control brings comfort, for we understand that everything unfolds in His perfect timing.

"There are many devices in a man's heart; nevertheless the counsel of the Lord, that shall stand" (Proverbs 19:21).

"And we know that all things work together for good to them that love God, to them who are the called according to his purpose" (Romans 8:28).

- **God is Always Good—I will not despair**—holding onto goodness in trials. Christianity doesn't promise an easy path. Times of despair often come when focus shifts away from God. Personal reflection reveals that despair is mitigated through prayer and recommitment to God's will. The act of focusing on the Lord is an anchor in turbulent times.

"We are afflicted in every way, but not crushed; perplexed, but not driven to despair; persecuted, but not forsaken; struck down, but not destroyed; always carrying in the body the death of Jesus, so that the life of Jesus may also be manifested in our bodies" (2 Corinthians 4:8–10).

- **God is Always Watching—I will not falter**—staying steadfast in observation. With the knowledge that God's gaze never leaves us, there's an inherent strength that comes with this understanding. It prompts a steady walk, one that does not stumble, for we know our actions and lives are constantly before the eyes of the Divine.

- **God is Always Victorious—I will not fail**—celebrating the ultimate triumph. In every challenge, the ultimate victory is assured for those who align with God's will. The assurance of God's perpetual triumph over all adversity is a powerful motivator to persist the persevere.

- **People who Believe in God's Promises will Experience Greater Blessings in their Lives**—experiencing the fullness of faith. Faith in God's promises opens the door to deeper spiritual experiences and blessings. The trust in these divine assurances elevates one's life beyond the immediate and the material, providing a perspective that sees and savors the greater workings of God's grace and purpose.

Each of these insights offers a framework for living that is rooted in spiritual truths. They direct us to a life that is not easily shaken, one that stands firm in the midst of trials, and confidently looks towards the promised victory and goodness of God. With these convictions, a believer is equipped to navigate the complexities of life while holding fast to the unwavering truths of God's Word and His nature.

Embrace His Watchfulness: Steadfastness in His Sight

Beneath the ever-watchful eyes of the Divine, you're not just observed—you're cherished, protected, and guided. Picture His gaze as a lighthouse beam, cutting through fog, leading ships safely to shore. In the same way, His watchfulness over you ensures that you never stray too far from the safety of His embrace. With every step you take, feel the assurance that His attention never wavers. Your journey isn't a solo endeavor; it's a joint venture with the Almighty as your vigilant partner.

- **The Joy of His Timing**—synchronized with the Divine. In the dance of life, God's timing is the perfect rhythm. When you move to the pulse of His divine timetable, you find that every step, every pivot, every leap happens with grace. It's not always about the speed but the synchronicity. When you feel out of step, remember His clock isn't broken—it's just set to a time zone that's beyond earthly understanding but always, always on time for your needs.

- **Savor His Endless Goodness**—an evergreen life. God's goodness isn't a fleeting season; it's an eternal spring. Imagine your life as a garden—every aspect of it tended by the Gardener whose green thumb brings forth color and life in the midst of any circumstance. In droughts, He is the rain; in darkness, He is the sun. Turn your face to His goodness, and let it color your world with an everlasting hue of hope and joy.

- **Trust His Unerring Plan**—peace in His purpose. The tapestry of our life is woven with threads of divine design. Each color, each thread, is selected with purpose and intention. Sometimes, it's only when you step back that you see the masterpiece that's being created. In the intricate design of your days, trust that He is crafting a narrative of beauty, resilience, and strength—a story that's uniquely yours, under the authorship of the greatest Storyteller.

- **Stand Firm in His Promises**—unshakable assurance. As you stand on the rock-solid promises of God, feel the firm ground beneath your feet. Every promise is a stone in the foundation of your faith—a fortress against the quaking uncertainties of the world. They are assurances that won't crumble, won't crack, and won't wear away with the wind of time.

- **Live in His Victory**—an invincible spirit. Embrace a spirit that's armored in the victory of Christ. Your battles are not just your own; they are already won. The triumph is not just for the skies above but for the ground you walk on every day. With every challenge faced, remember that you're enveloped in the victory of the cross—a victory that doesn't promise an absence of conflict but the ultimate win over it.

- **Bask in His Blessings**—a life overflowing. Let your heart be a vessel into which God pours His blessings—so full that it overflows, spilling over into the lives of others. Your life is not a cup half empty or half full; it's briming with the outpouring of His grace, love, and mercy. Drink deeply from this wellspring of blessings, and let the overflow be a testament to the abundance He promises.

In the grand symphony of life, you are an instrument tuned by His promises. Play your notes with confidence, and let the music speak of His faithfulness. The crescendo is building, the melody is unwavering, and the Composer is none other than God Himself. Step into the melody of His promises, and let your life be a song of praise, a harmonic echo of His eternal love and faithfulness.

Harness His Unfailing Strength: Courage in Your Convictions

With God as your unfaltering source of strength, approach each day with the courage of a lion. The road ahead may twist and turn, but your convictions are rooted in something deeper than the soil of this earth—they are anchored in the Divine. Just as a tree stands firm against the howling winds, your spirit is bolstered by the might of His Word, unwavering and resolute.

- **Flourish in His Constant Care**—thrive in His presence. Imagine yourself as a greenhouse bloom, basking in the constant, nurturing presence of the Gardener. His care is meticulous and tender, tailored to your every need. In this greenhouse, there is no withering—only flourishing. Your leaves stretch towards the warmth of His love, and your colors shine bright with vitality. God's presence is the sunlight under which you grow, not just survive, but truly thrive.

- **Celebrate His Infinite Wisdom**—enlightened paths ahead. Every experience is steeped in the wisdom of the Almighty. With each decision you face, envisage His wisdom as a lantern, illuminating the path at your feet. Where there is uncertainty, His wisdom casts out shadows, revealing a way forward that leads to enlightenment and understanding. Our journey is not a wander in the dark but a walk in the light of His profound insight.

- **Rejoice in His Unending Love**—unconditional and all-encompassing. Dwell in the comfort of God's love—a love that knows no bounds, no conditions, no end. Picture it as an ocean, vast and unfathomable, enveloping you with waves of comfort and warmth. In the ebb and flow of life, His love is the tide that always returns to you, gentle and reassuring. No matter how far you drift, His love is an anchor, forever holding you close to His heart.

- **Trust in His Omnipotent Power**—a foundation of faith. Stand in awe of His omnipotent power, the bedrock of your faith. It's not just a belief—it's a knowing as certain as the ground beneath your feet and the sky above your head. His power is the pulse of all creation, the force that weaves the fabric of the universe, and the very breath in your lungs. With each beat of your heart, remember the Might that orchestrates existence itself resides with you.

- **Draw Near to His Unceasing Mercy**—a well of forgiveness. Bathe in the well of God's mercy, where forgiveness flows like a never-ending stream. In moments of faltering, when you stumble and fall, His mercy is there to cleanse, to renew, and to restore. It's not a finite resource—it's as abundant as the air you breathe and as constant as the stars that pierce the night sky.

- **Engage with His Living Word**—active and alive. Engage with the Bible, not as a static text, but as the living, breathing Word of God. Let it be as real and active as the beating of your heart, as dynamic as the thoughts that dance in your mind. For within its pages lies the vibrancy of truth, the stories that resonate with your own, and the promises that are alive—echoing through time to guide, to heal, and to transform.

Every sunrise is a canvas painted with His promises, every sunset a reminder of His faithfulness. With every breath you take, let the reality of His promises fill you with a hope that shines brighter than the morning star. In this divine dance with the Creator, your life becomes an expression of His ceaseless love—a portrait of grace that speaks of His glory to a world in need of hope. Step into each day as a living testament to the promises of God, for in His Word, you find the strength to face the morrow, the joy to embrace the present, and the hope to dream of a future wrapped in His unfailing love.

Embrace His Unchanging Truth: Stability in Every Storm

In the storms of life, His truth is the anchor that holds steadfast. Imagine yourself amidst turbulent waves, the sky overhead churning with uncertainty. Yet, in your hand is a compass—His unchanging truth. It doesn't spin wildly; it points ever towards true North. No squall can unsettle its direction; no tempest can lead it astray. Take heart in the knowledge that His promises are the same yesterday, today, and forever.

- **Savor His Perfect Peace**—a tranquil refuge. Picture His peace as a serene garden, a quiet refuge away from the chaos of the world. As you step into this garden, the stillness surrounds you like a soft cloak. The birds sing songs of serenity, the trees sway gently to the rhythm of His grace. Here, in the divine stillness, your heart finds the rhythm of calm, and your soul sings with the harmony of His perfect peace.

- **Relish in His Joyous Celebration**—jubilation in belief. Allow your heart to dance in the celebration of His joy. It's not a muted joy, confined to the corner of your being—it's a jubilant, resounding exclamation of belief. Every moment you live in His promises is a note in an eternal symphony, a step in an everlasting dance. Let your life be a festival of His love, where every day is a jubilee, and every breath is an anthem of joy.

- **Bask in His Divine Presence**—a constant companion. Embrace the notion that you are never alone, for His presence is a constant companion in your journey. It's a presence that doesn't overshadow but gently accompanies. In the quiet moments, in the bustling intersections of life, feel the reassuring touch of the Divine walking with you. Your shadow is not just a silhouette on the ground; it's a reminder that He is always by your side.

- **Absorb His Timeless Wisdom**—a guiding star. Lean on His wisdom, a guiding star in the vast sky of existence. When the night of confusion envelops you, look up and find the star that never dims. Its light is His wisdom, timeless and profound, a celestial guide on your voyage through life. In the darkness, it beckons with a gentle glow, leading you to dawn's light on the horizon.

- **Reflect His Boundless Generosity**—a life of giving. Live your life as a mirror reflecting His boundless generosity. You have been blessed not merely to contain these blessings but to let them overflow. Like a cup filled to the brim, let His love and grace spill over the edges, reaching out to touch the lives of others. In giving, you embody the essence of His character, and through you, His generosity is made manifest in the world.

In the tapestry of life, each thread is woven with His promises. Your story is interlaced with His eternal truths, a pattern that unfolds with the beauty of His design. As you step forth, do so with the assurance that the weaver is none other than the Creator Himself. Your life, a vibrant thread in His masterpiece, is a witness to the world of the steadfast promises of God. Carry forth this message, live out this truth, and revel in the abundance of His eternal love.

As you apply this fifth step, may your life be a testament to the promises of God, a living tapestry woven with threads of divine truth that display the grand design He has authored for you.

Step Six
Living the Zoe Life
The Essence of True Discipleship

18

The transformation was both profound and exhilarating. As I delved deeper into my renewed commitment to the Divine, the blessings that began to manifest in my life were beyond anything I had ever known. This wasn't merely an existence; it was a vibrant, pulsating "zoe" life. Derived from ancient Greek, the term "zoe" transcends the ordinary understanding of life. It signifies a life that's genuine, teeming with vigor, and entirely devoted to God—a life that originates directly from the Creator Himself.

Delving into the profound etymology of "zoe," one uncovers layers of meaning. On the one hand, it denotes the span of an individual's life on earth, as expressed in scriptures like Luke 16:25 and James 4:14:

"But Abraham said, 'Child, remember that you in your lifetime received your good things, and Lazarus in like manner bad things; but now he is comforted here, and you are in anguish'" (Luke 16:25).

"Yet you do not know what tomorrow will bring. What is your life? For you are a mist that appears for a little time and then vanishes" (James 4:14).

Yet, in the vast tapestry of the Greek New Testament, "zoe" embodies a more profound significance. It celebrates the life God bestows upon believers through Christ. Often paired with the term "eon," it reflects the eternal, everlasting essence of life—one that stretches beyond the realm of time and space.

The scriptures eloquently proclaim:

"Fight the good fight of faith, lay hold on eternal life, whereunto you are also called, and have professed a good profession before many witnesses" (1 Timothy 6:12).

Embracing the "zoe" life isn't about fleeting moments of spirituality. It's a perpetual dance of the soul with the Divine. I don't wear the cloak of Christianity occasionally; it's interwoven into the very fabric of my being. My faith is not reserved for Sunday sermons or moments of despair. It's the air I breathe, the song my heart sings. With the Holy Spirit residing within, fear and worldly anxieties dissolve, replaced by an unshakeable peace. My conversations with Jesus aren't scheduled—they're as spontaneous as they are continuous. He is my ever-present companion, guiding every step and decision.

Living a genuine "zoe" life means acknowledging God's omnipresence. He knows where I am, and His plans for me are grander than any I could devise. I've learned that by surrendering to His ways— eschewing my own desires and inclinations—I'm ushered toward my true destiny: an eternal communion with Him. In this earthly realm, He has graciously led me to Coeur d'Alene, Idaho—a dream residence that I fondly term "temporary." Because in the grander scheme, our ultimate home, filled with infinite wonders and blessings, lies in the embrace of Heaven. The journey is ongoing, a continuous exploration, and with each day, I revel in the myriad blessings that unfold.

The Sixth Step to Unveiling Your Destiny: Living the Zoe Life

Discipleship in the Christian sense is the process of leading someone to become Christ-like. The disciple of Christ is to become like Christ in everything. The primary purpose of Jesus' first coming to the world was to establish the Kingdom of God through his death.

> Jesus said, "Therefore whosoever hears these sayings of mine, and does them, I will liken him unto a wise man, which built his house upon a rock: And the rain descended, and the floods came, and the winds blew, and beat upon that house; and it fell not: for it was founded on a rock. And every one that hears these sayings of mine, and does them not, will be likened unto a foolish man, which built his house upon the sand: And the rain descended, and the floods came, and the winds blew, and

beat upon that house; and it fell: and great was the fall of it" (Matthew 7:24–27).

Apostle Paul said, "Wherefore I beseech (beg) you, be you followers of me" (1 Corinthians 4:16).

Apostle Paul said, "Be you followers of me, even as I also am (an example) of Christ" (1 Corinthians 11:1).

Apostle Paul said, "Brethren, be followers together of me, and mark them which walk so as you have us for an example" (1 Philippians 3:17).

Apostle John said, "Beloved, follow not that which is evil, but that which is good. He that does good is of God: but he that does evil has not seen God" (3 John 1:11).

In the Bible, Christ's final command to His followers is to "Therefore, as you go, disciple people in all nations, baptizing them in the name of the Father, and the Son, and the Holy Spirit" (Matthew 28:19). The Christian church has taken this command very seriously, but what does it mean to the new Christians? What does it mean to be a disciple of Christ, much less to make more disciples?

- **Real Discipleship**—becoming Christ-like. To truly embrace discipleship, we delve into a life where Christ's teachings aren't just inscribed in the margins of our lives, but they become the very lines upon which our stories are written. Discipleship is the canvas upon which the colors of our character, actions, and intentions blend to mirror the image of Christ Himself.

- **Laying Foundations**—building on the Rock. The vivid illustration given by Jesus about building a house on the rock serves as a foundational truth for discipleship. It teaches us that hearing His Words is not enough; we must act upon them. To live the "zoe life"—a life of divine quality and vitality—means laying down every brick of our existence upon the bedrock of His teachings. It is in the doing, not just the hearing, that our spiritual edifices withstand life's relentless storms.

- **Following Paul's Footsteps**—emulating apostolic example. Apostle Paul's invitation to follow him as he follows Christ isn't a call to mimicry but a call to a genuine transformation that reflects in our very being. It's about walking a path so closely aligned with Paul's that our journeys become indistinguishable from his example—an example that ultimately points to Christ. As we navigate through the complexities of life, keeping our eyes on such examples helps us stay true to the course of discipleship.

- **Embracing John's Counsel**—choosing good over evil. Apostle John simplifies the pursuit of discipleship to a fundamental choice: to follow good or evil. To embody discipleship is to choose goodness, to choose God, at every fork in the road. It is not merely an abstract concept but a daily, active decision that aligns us more closely with the divine nature.

- **The Great Commission**—discipling nations. Christ's Great Commission to disciple nations expands the scope of discipleship beyond personal transformation to a global mission. It calls us to not only live as disciples but also to be vessels through which others can encounter the transformative power of Christ. It's a call to be spiritual mentors, to baptize not just with water, but with the depth of the Gospel that touches and changes hearts.

- **Practical discipleship**—applying the Blueprint to Your Life.

  1. **Immerse Yourself in the Word**. Become so familiar with His teachings that they become your first language, the lens through which you view the world.

  2. **Act on His Teachings**. Find ways every day to live out the beatitudes, to embody the fruits of the Spirit, and to serve others as if serving Christ Himself.

  3. **Mentorship and Community**. Seek out spiritual mentors like Paul and join communities that challenge and encourage you to grow in faith.

  4. **Lead by Example**. Let your life be a testimony to your discipleship. Just as John advocated, let your good works and your fight against evil speak of the God you serve.

  5. **Embrace the Mission**. Find your place in the Great Commission. Whether it's through evangelism, acts of service, or living a life that draws others to Christ, participate in the global calling to make disciples.

  6. **Continuous Growth**. Understand that discipleship is a journey, not a destination. Commit to lifelong learning, growing, and becoming more like Christ every day.

In a world yearning for authenticity, the disciple who walks the talk becomes a beacon of hope and a testament to the transformative power of Christ. By becoming like Christ in everything, we light the way for others to follow. The "zoe life" is then not just for us to live but for us to share, multiplying the disciples of Christ in a world that desperately needs His light.

Embrace this calling with a heart full of courage and a spirit willing to journey, and remember, the essence of true discipleship is found in the footsteps of the One we follow. It is a life lived in the fullness of Christ's love, a blueprint not just for a sturdy structure, but for a vibrant, awe-inspiring cathedral that stands as a testament to the Master Builder.

Changing From the Inside Out

Christian discipleship—the inner transformation of a disciple—transcends the mere acquisition of knowledge; it's a metamorphosis that begins when one takes the leap of faith. This transformative process is the cornerstone of a life built on Christ's teachings. When we open our hearts to Jesus as our Savior, a remarkable change starts to take place within us—our spiritual DNA is rewritten by His loving hands.

How God reshapes us from within:

- **Immersing in the Word**. By reading the Bible, we start to grasp the essence of Jesus' life and His call to put Him above all else (Mark 8:34–38). It's in this daily devotion that we understand what it means to live a life modeled after His.

- **Guidance of the Holy Spirit**. We learn to attune our ears to the gentle whispers of the Holy Spirit, our indwelling guide, who empowers us to shun temptation and soar above trials (Ephesians 6:10–18).

- **Self-Examination**. The practice of reflecting on our thoughts, actions, and words against the Scriptures molds us into doers of the Word, not merely its auditors (James 1:22).

- **Abiding in Christ**. In abiding, we allow the Holy Spirit to cultivate the fruits of the Spirit within us—a divine harvest that sprouts from within and is not of our own making (Galatians 5:22–23).

- **Loving through Action**. We begin to demonstrate love not just in emotion, but in deeds, reflecting the love of Jesus (John 13:35).

- **Spreading the Faith**. There grows within us an insatiable desire to share the transformative narrative of our faith with others (1 Peter 3:15).

Discipleship is a journey that starts with small steps—the journey from follower to disciple-maker. It's not a sprint but a marathon. God doesn't call the equipped; He equips the called, guiding us from fledgling believers to mature disciples capable of mentoring others. The notion of making disciples should not intimidate us. Instead, it should invigorate us with a sense of purpose and possibility.

Discipleship is faith. At the heart of discipleship lies unwavering faith—faith that God will not abandon those who earnestly seek Him (Psalm 9:10). With God, we unearth the strength to not only become disciples but also to create new ones, sharing the light of faith.

Discipleship is living a purpose-driven life for God. To live a life that's Christ-centered is to understand the essence of glorifying God in every aspect of our existence. It's about seeking a legacy that echoes into eternity, making an impact that transcends the fleeting allure of worldly pursuits. Rick Warren's "The Purpose Drive Life" distills this into five divine purposes that outline a blueprint for a meaningful life:

- **Real Worship**. We exist to delight God, our lives a continuous act of worship.

- **Real Fellowship**. We are called to experience life together as part of God's family.

- **Real Discipleship**. We are on a transformative journey to become more like Christ.

- **Real Ministry**. We are shaped to serve, turning our gifts into acts of genuine care.

- **Real Evangelism**. We are agents of the Good News, tasked to share it with the world.

For a profound dive into these purposes, Rick Warren's TED talk, "A Life of Purpose," incapsulates the essence of living a life that truly matters, a life that not only resonates with our own souls but also reverberates through the lives of others.

Embarking on the path of discipleship is to accept the call to be reshaped from the inside out, embracing a transformation that is both deeply personal and expansively influential. It's a call to a life lived in full alignment with the heart of God, a journey that in every step is a dance of grace, truth, and boundless love.

Embracing the Zoe Life: The God-Kind of Life

The "zoe life" is more than mere existence. When we talk about the "zoe life" in Christian discipleship, we're referring to something extraordinary and profound. This isn't just life as we typically know it— the everyday cycle of waking and sleeping, eating and working. The "zoe life" is the God-kind of life; it's about quality, not just quantity. It's a rich tapestry of spiritual vitality that Jesus promised:

"I have come that they may have life, and have it to the full" (John 10:10).

Characteristics of the "zoe life":

- **Everlasting Connection**. "Zoe life" is eternal life. It starts the moment you embrace Christ and continues forever. It transcends time, not waiting for the afterlife but beginning here and now.

- **Abundant Nature**. The "zoe life" is not measured by the breaths we take but by the moments that take our breath away. It's about living abundantly, with a heart overflowing with God's love, grace, and power.

- **Transformative Impact**. Those who live the "zoe life" experience transformation that radiates outward. They become beacons of hope, love, and peace in a world desperate for the light of Christ.

Living the "zoe life": Imagine waking up each day knowing you're infused with Divine life. Your heartbeat syncs with the heartbeat of God; your steps are aligned with His purpose. This is the "zoe life"—

where every mundane task can become an act of worship, every interaction an opportunity to display God's love.

The daily walk in the "zoe life":

1. **Prayer as Oxygen**. In the "zoe life," prayer is like breathing—essential and life-giving. It's our direct line to the Father, a conversation that never has to end.

2. **Word as Nourishment**. Just as we need food to live, we need the Word to thrive in the "zoe life." It sustains us, strengthens us, and equips us for every good work.

3. **Community as Family**. We're not meant to walk the "zoe life" alone. Our brothers and sisters in Christ are our co-travelers, supporting us, cheering us on, and sometimes carrying us through tough times.

4. **Service as Lifestyle**. Service isn't just something we do; it's a way of life. The "zoe life" compels us to serve joyfully, giving of ourselves as Christ gave Himself for us.

5. **Evangelism as Privilege**. Sharing our faith isn't a duty; it's a privilege. In the "zoe life," we're so full of what God has done for us that we can't help but spill over into the lives of others.

Dare to dive deep into the "zoe life." It's not about a spiritual elite; it's for every child of God. It's not a special offer, limited to a select few—it's part of your inheritance in Christ. When you choose to live the "zoe life," you choose to step into a reality that's charged with divine purpose and potential.

The "zoe life" isn't about waiting for heaven; it's about bringing heaven to earth through our lives—the "zoe life" and You. It's about seeing God's kingdom come, His will be done, on earth as it is in heaven—through you, through me, through us.

So, take a breath, take a step, and embrace the "zoe life." Let it transform you, let it define you, and let it radiate through you to touch a world in need. This is your calling, your destiny, and your journey. Live it out loud, live it with joy, live it with "zoe!"

Step Seven
The Sacred Journey of Purposeful Evangelism

19

Unveiling the divine tapestry of my life, I found that the thread that held everything together, the core of God's design for me, was evangelism. But not just any evangelism—God had a unique vision, a distinct role, crafted especially for me. This wasn't a generic call to spread His word; it was a personalized invitation to play a pivotal role in His grand narrative.

Often, when one thinks of evangelism, images of preachers on pulpits or missionaries in far-off lands come to mind. But for me, the Lord's directive was different. It was innovative, contemporary, and tailored to my innate gifts and passions. With the tools He provided—The Ridge Publishing Group's vast array of books, instructive textbooks, visually compelling print documentaries, engaging board games, and evocative card decks—I was equipped to evangelize in a manner that was unprecedented. Every creation was an ode to His majesty, a celebration of His boundless love. Each time I heard the echoes of "Hallelujah!" in response, my heart swelled with gratitude.

The Bible resonates with this sentiment, declaring:

"For we are His handiwork, intricately designed in Christ Jesus to perform noble deeds, acts which God has meticulously planned in advance for us to embark upon" (Ephesians 2:10).

This scripture encapsulates the essence of my divine calling. It is not by accident or coincidence; it is by His intentional and masterful design.

Now, the path I've trodden is not just my tale to tell. It's a blueprint, a guiding star, for others seeking clarity in their purpose. As we journey through this seventh step of seven steps—your blueprint for a meaningful life—we see a beautiful pattern unfolded. A pattern that doesn't merely skim the surface of a Christian life but delves deep, immersing oneself fully in the embrace of the Lord. Each step acts as a beacon, illuminating the path to discovering and honoring God's unique plan for you.

For, in understanding and embracing our purpose, we don't just fulfill our personal destinies—we become instruments of His will, resonating with His love, and leading others towards the light of salvation. Your journey of purposeful evangelism awaits; are you ready to uncover the secret treasures God has set aside for you?

The Seventh Step to Unveiling Your Destiny: Live Out Real Evangelism

Dear reader, envision yourself as a beacon of hope, a vessel through which the love and message of Christ flows boundlessly. This is the essence of evangelism—not a task, not a box to check, but a sacred journey you embark on every day of your life.

- **Evangelism—Sharing, Not Shoving**. Evangelism is often misunderstood. It's not about shoving religion down someone's throat; it's about sharing the greatest love story ever told. It's the art of conversation, where you speak less about religion and more about relationship—your personal relationship with God.

- **Begin with Your Story—It's Powerful**. Your journey, your transformation, your moments of doubt and triumph—these are the narratives that resonate with the human heart. Start with what God has done in your life. Your story could be the key that unlocks someone else's prison.

- **Everyday Evangelism—Make It a Lifestyle**.

  1. **Presence Over Preaching**. Sometimes, it's your presence, not your preaching, that heralds the Gospel loudest. Live a life that beckons others to ask, "What's the source of your hope?"

  2. **Kindness as a Conversation Starter**. A simple act of kindness can open doors for deeper discussions. Let your compassion draw people in and pave the way for meaningful dialogue.

3. **Active Listening as a Ministry**. Real evangelism involves listening—truly listening—to people's stories, struggles, and questions without judgment.

4. **Invitations to Experience Christ**. Invite friends to church, yes, but also to see Christ in your home, in your friendships, in your daily actions.

- **Build Bridges, not Walls**. We're called to be bridge-builders, connecting people to God. This isn't about constructing theological barriers; it's about paving a path to the Savior.

- **Use Your Talents in Service to Others**. God has gifted you uniquely—maybe you're a listener, a speaker, an artist, or a thinker. Whatever your gift, use it to demonstrate God's love. Your talent is a tool for evangelism.

- **The Ripple Effect—One Life at a Time**. Never underestimate the impact of planting a single seed of faith. It can create ripples that extend far beyond what you can see. One life touched by God through you can lead to a family, a community, a nation transformed.

- **The Ultimate Reward**. Remember, the ultimate goal of evangelism isn't to rack up conversations like sales but to genuinely love others as Christ loves them. And in doing so, you'll find the deep joy and satisfaction that comes from fulfilling your purpose.

- **Embrace the Journey**. As you step out today, and every day, on this sacred journey of purposeful evangelism, do so with the confidence that you carry the most precious message known to humankind—the Gospel of Jesus Christ. Be bold, be brave, be loving, and watch as the masterful hand of God weaves your efforts into His grand tapestry of redemption. This is your calling, your sacred journey—live it out with passion and purpose!

The Living Testimony: You Are the Message

You, dear reader, are the "living epistle" known and read by all men (2 Corinthians 3:2). Your life is the message. Your actions, your joy in trials, your peace in turmoil—they all preach the vibrant, living reality of the Gospel. When you walk into a room, you bring more than just yourself; you carry the very essence of the Holy Spirit's presence.

- **The "Zoe Life"—Vibrant Evangelism**. The "zoe life," the God-kind of life, is not just for you to live in abundance but to share abundantly. It's infectious, it's compelling, it's the kind of life that makes people stop in their tracks and wonder what the source of your vitality is.

- **Creating Moments that Matter**. Every encounter is an opportunity for evangelism. From the barista who makes your coffee to the colleague struggling with life's burdens, every person you meet is a divine appointment. Create moments that matter, that speak to the hearts of individuals.

- **A Legacy of Faith**. Consider the legacy you want to leave. Is it not a trail of hope, a series of footprints leading straight to the Cross? Your mission field is where you are right now—your workplace, your school, your community.

- **Equip Yourself with Knowledge and Wisdom**. Equipping yourself with the knowledge and wisdom found in the Scriptures is vital. Understand the core of what you believe and be ready to gently and respectfully explain your hope to anyone who asks (1 Peter 3:15).

- **Connect, Don't Condemn**. Our mission is to connect, not to condemn. We're called to show the way to the bridge, not to push someone over it. Christ's love compels us to move with grace and truth.

- **The Power of Prayer in Evangelism**. Never underestimate the power of prayer in evangelism. Pray for the hearts of those you encounter. Pray for openness, for divine moments, and for your words to be seasoned with grace.

- **The Harvest is Plentiful—Be the laborer**. The fields are ripe for harvest (John 4:25). Will you be the laborer who steps out in faith? Remember the harvest is God's; you are merely the hands and feet, serving obediently.

- **Evangelism as Worship**. Lastly, see evangelism as an act of worship. It is a response to the greatness of God and His love for us. Let this reverent act flow naturally from your devotion and love for Him.

In this walk of faith, as you live out the essence of purposeful evangelism, remember it's not the size of your audience but the sincerity of your testimony. Whether you touch one life or one thousand, it's invaluable in the eyes of the Lord. Go forth, dear reader, with courage and love, and live out this sacred journey of evangelism with the assurance that God is with you, every step of the way.

Embark On the Sacred Journey

Imagine your life as a beacon, not just a simple light but a lighthouse guiding ships through stormy seas to safe harbor. That's evangelism—guiding souls to the safety of God's love.

- **Live Out Your Testimony**. Your story is unique, and it's a testament to God's work in your life. Share it! There's someone out there who needs to hear exactly what you've been through and how God has brought you out of darkness into His marvelous light.

- **Serve with Love**. Service is a language of love that everyone understands. When you serve others, you're not just doing a good deed; you're showing them God's love in action. This opens doors for deeper conversations about faith.

- **Be Authentic**. People aren't looking for perfection; they're seeking authenticity. Be real about your struggles and how your faith has shaped your journey. Authenticity breeds trust, and trust opens the gateway to the soul.

- **Practice Intentional Listening**. Listening is one of the most powerful tools in evangelism. It shows that you value the person and are genuinely interested in their life. Through active listening, you can discern needs and offer hope.

- **Invest in Relationships**. Evangelism isn't a one-time event; it's a lifelong journey of investing in relationships. Show consistent care and concern. It's through ongoing relationships that people will see Christ in you.

- **Be the Example**. Lead by example. Let your life be such that people want to know the reason for your hope. When your life reflects Christ, people will be drawn to the light of His presence within you.

- **Walk in Humility**. Remember, it's not about winning arguments but guiding souls to Christ. Walk humbly, knowing it's the Holy Spirit's work to convict and the grace of God to save.

- **Encourage with Scripture**. The Word of God is alive and powerful. Encourage others with scriptures that have strengthened you. Sometimes, the most profound impact can come from sharing a simple verse that speaks to the heart.

- **Celebrate Every Step**. Celebrate every step someone takes towards God, no matter how small. Rejoice with the angels over one sinner who repents. Every step is progress in this sacred journey.

- **Keep the Faith**. There will be challenges, rejections, and days of doubt, but keep the faith. The seeds you plant today may blossom in ways you will never see. Trust God's process.

As you commit to this seventh step, let your life be a vivid illustration of God's transforming power. Purposeful evangelism is not just about speaking the right words but living a life that echoes them. Go forth with a heart full of God's love and eyes open to the opportunities He provides. Be ready, for you are on the sacred journey of purposeful evangelism, where every encounter could change a life forever.

Afterword

As we turn the final page of "Total Surrender: My Story and Your Blueprint for a Meaningful Life," it is my sincere wish that these chapters have not merely been read, but experienced; they have resonated with you, spoken to your heart, and ignited a flame of introspection and ambition within your soul.

Part One: Total Surrender, My Story was an odyssey through the landscapes of my own vulnerabilities and victories. With every anecdote and reflection, I sought to lay bare the essence of a life immersed in the pursuit of truth, a life that has been both blessed and sanctified by the touch of the Divine. It is a chronicle of transformation through faith, a narrative built upon the cornerstone of unwavering trust in a higher purpose—God's plan.

Through the recounting of trials weathered and lessons learned, this section was meant to act as a bridge connecting our shared human experiences, encouraging you to see the echoes of your own journey in mine. It was about revealing that within the symphony of our lives, every note of sorrow and joy plays a crucial role in the divine composition.

Part Two: Total Surrender, Your Blueprint for a Meaningful Life, then transitioned from the story of one to the empowerment of many. It was an invitation to weave the threads of wisdom gleaned from one life into the tapestry of countless others. The seven steps outlined are more than directives; they are the seven pillars upon which a life of purpose is built. Each step, from understanding true faith to embodying purposeful evangelism, was designed to be a stepping stone on your journey towards a more profound destiny.

In this era, often characterized by many as the "last days" or "end times," where the drumbeats of prophecy seem to resonate with increasing intensity, the message of this book aims to be both a solace and call to action. It seeks to instill a sense of urgency, not for fear of what is to come, but for the love of what can be accomplished when a life is wholly dedicated to the pursuit of truth and service.

The path of total surrender is not one of passive resignation, but of active engagement with the world. It is a declaration that life, in all its complexity and mystery, is to be embraced and not merely endured. With each act of surrender, we are not relinquishing our power; we are reclaiming it, aligning our will with the infinite and making ourselves conduits for miracles.

As you embark on the next leg of your journey, take with you the certainties and the uncertainties, the peace and the passion, the stillness and the storm. Hold onto the truth that surrender is not the abdication of strength; it is its ultimate expression. Know that in the hands of the Divine, your stories are not ending but are being continuously written, each chapter more compelling than the last.

AFTERWORD

May the path of surrender lead you to waters of renewal and to the mountaintops of revelation. May the blueprint you hold not only guide you but also become a beacon for others who wander in search of light.

In the end, our stories are not merely our own; they are a legacy, a testament, and a gift to the world. So, may your life be a testament to the beauty of surrender, and may your legacy be one of hope, inspiration, and unwavering faith.

Let me leave you with these scriptures:

"God saved you by His grace when you believed. And you can't take credit for this; it is a gift from God. Salvation is not a reward for the good things we have done, so none of us can boast about it—for we are God's masterpiece. He has created us anew in Christ Jesus, so we can do the good things He planned for us long ago" (Ephesians 2:8–10).

"We are not saved merely for our own benefit but to serve Christ and build up the church—believers are the church" (Ephesians 4:12).

God bless you.

TOTAL SURRENDER

Author Photo © 2023 Edwin Wolfe

LORI ANN MOESZINGER also known as simply "L" is the face behind The Ridge Publishing Group and its imprints. She is an American author, blogger, and publisher who resides in Coeur d'Alene, Idaho, with her husband and two dogs. She writes under the pseudonyms: Ann Patterson for her business law pieces; L. A. Moeszinger for her writing, publishing, and marketing pieces; Lori Ann Moeszinger for her biblical books and personal pieces; and a handful of others for her series, The Manhattan Diaries. She believes strongly in faith, blessings, and working her butt off . . . and she thinks one of the best things about being an author-publisher—unlike the lawyer she used to be—is that she can let her passion out.

Transcending her former life as a lawyer, Lori now revels in the freedom of expression that authorship and publishing afford—a stark contrast to the rigid confines of law. Her new chapter is one marked by a fervent passion for empowering others, a commitment to hard work, and the joy of sharing her literary gifts.

Discover the multifaced worlds Lori has woven at her websites and blog sites, or connect with her on her social media platforms where she continues to inspire, educate, and transform the written word into a shared experience of growth and discovery.

Parent Website: https://www.RidgePublishingGroup.com and

blog site https://www.PublisherAndHerWorld.com

Publisher Website: https://www.GuardiansofBiblicalTruth.com and

blog site https://www.Jesus-Says.com

Author website: https://www.LAMoeszinger.com and New Youniversity sites:

https://www.NewYouniversity.com, https://www.ManhattanChronicles.com

Bridge Website: https://www.AuthorsDoor.com and

blog site https://www.AuthorsRedDoor.com

Entertainment website: https://www.EthanFoxBooks.com and

blog site https://www.KidsStagram.com

Want More?

Welcome to Coffee with God! Jesus-Says! Dive into our blog for inspiring insights and biblical truths that deepen your faith and enrich your spiritual journey. Explore thought-provoking articles, personal testimonies, and practical guidance rooted in Scripture. Whether you're new to the faith or a lifelong believer, Jesus-Says.com offers wisdom and encouragement for your walk with Christ. Join our community and grow in your relationship with God!

Guardians of Biblical Truth Hub

Welcome to our Guardians of Biblical Truth Facebook page! Join our community to deepen your understanding of the Bible and live out its principles. Engage in enriching Bible studies, share faith testimonies, and connect with like-minded believers. Whether you're new to the faith or a seasoned believer, you'll find support and inspiration here. Join us and grow in your walk with Christ.

Guardians of Biblical Truth Forum

Welcome to our Guardians of Biblical Truth Forum! Join our closed Facebook group to deepen your understanding of the Bible and strengthen your faith. Engage in enriching discussions, share personal testimonies, and connect with a supportive community of believers. Whether you're new to the faith or a seasoned believer, you'll find inspiration and encouragement here. Join us today and grow in your walk with Christ!

www.ingramcontent.com/pod-product-compliance
Lightning Source LLC
Chambersburg PA
CBHW021626120626
46545CB00002B/418